**Public Policy for Day Care
of Young Children**

Published in cooperation with The Urban Institute, Washington, D.C.

Public Policy for Day Care of Young Children

Organization, Finance, and Planning

Dennis R. Young† and Richard R. Nelson††
with contributions by

Richard B. Zamoff, The Urban Institute
Emma L. Jackson, Florida State University
Jerolyn R. Lyle, American University
Michael Krashinsky, Yale University

†Program for Urban and Policy Sciences, State University of New York and the Urban Institute, Washington, D.C.

††Department of Economics, Yale University

Lexington Books
D.C. Heath and Company
Lexington, Massachusetts
Toronto   London

Library of Congress Cataloging in Publication Data

Young, Dennis, 1943—
   Public policy for day care of young children: organization, finance and
planning.

   1. Day nurseries—United States.   2. Day nurseries—United States—
Finance.   3. Federal aid to day nurseries—United States.   I. Nelson, R.,
joint author.   II. Title.
HV854.Y68   362.7'1   73-6792
IBSN 0-669-85514-6

Published simultaneously in Canada.

Printed in the United States of America.

International Standard Book Number: 0-669-85514-6

Library of Congress Catalog Card Number: 73-6792

Contents

List of Figure and Tables

viii

Foreword

In recent years public policy concerning the care of young children has stimulated a major national dialogue. The authors of *Public Policy for Day Care of Young Children: Organization, Finance, and Planning* have enriched the dialogue. They use, as a point of departure, the observation that "Social intervention . . . has been motivated by the understanding that our children of today will be tomorrow's adults, and that rearing children is society's most important investment in the future."

This volume is an important contribution, since the literature on day care has primarily come from workers in the child development and human services professions. Such literature is rich in observations of child development and the problems of intervention programs. But there has been virtually no literature on the administration of these programs. Fortunately, the authors' awareness of the programmatic issues is sensitive and sophisticated as they elucidate the public policy and administrative issues. For this, workers in the field of day care can be grateful, for they have been trying to wend their way through the complexities of planning, organizing, and evaluating programs without the ready resource material which is contained in this volume.

The reasons why day care has become a highly visible issue is described as reflecting a variety of problems of interest to distinct and disparate groups. Three major concerns—the three "w's"—working mothers, women's liberation, and welfare—are dealt with in detail. It is refreshing to have a presentation by a group which deals effectively with the broad national aspects of the problem while at the same time presents data on studies which they carried out in the District of Columbia. These studies provide practical suggestions for groups at the local level as well as for the policy and decision makers.

The reader will find the presentations well balanced while presenting a point of view. In the section on financing, the suggestion is made that any subsidy for services be tied to the child rather than to the supplier of services. There is also a comprehensive discussion of the problems of operating day care on a proprietary basis. Among other aspects of quality control, the necessity for public scrutiny of programs is emphasized—or specifically the authors state, "Day care centers must operate in a fish bowl."

All workers in the field of day care struggle with the allocation of resources: the quantity-quality trade-off problems. The treatment of this problem and the related one, the tension between welfare-oriented and child-focused sources of support and their policy conflicts are treated fully. We will continue to struggle with the policy problems of serving the many children and families in need of services and the difficulties in maintaining high quality standards for the services. Since resources are finite, we will need to learn to make these policy decisions more judiciously and effectively in the interests of children and families. The summary of issues and options in this volume should help us in fulfilling our responsibilities.

Since we have had a burst of publications on the child developmental aspects of day care, workers have ready reference materials for curriculum planning and evaluation for good quality developmentally-oriented day care. This volume should serve as a companion piece to help us through the organizational, financing and planning aspects which are no less significant. There is also included an up-to-date presentation of recent legislative trends and their complexity. We can be grateful to the authors for the broad range of coverage, the lucidity of the writing, and its brevity which should increase its readership. Its result should be better informed legislators, public officials, administrators and child development workers which should lead to improved programs of care for our young children as we shape policy and programs in the years to come.

Julius B. Richmond, M.D.
Director, Judge Baker Guidance Center
Boston, Massachusetts

Preface

Authors often employ a provocative quotation to begin their works. We would like to have done this here, but the task of selection is particularly difficult on the subject of day care for young children. One problem is that the term *day care* is commonly applied over a wide range of services including temporary babysitting operations, informal custodial care of children in neighbors' homes, formal institutional care, and preschool education in day care centers and nursery schools. For our purposes we would narrow the search to writers or speakers concerned with the more formal day care arrangements, where matters of public policy and subsidy are most directly involved. But even within this context, those interested in day care span a broad spectrum of philosophies, opinions, and interests with respect to the purposes of day care services. Hence, one is faced with a dilemma: should one quote a spokeswoman for women's liberation, a speaker concerned with the welfare problem, or an advocate of child development and preschool education? Any choice is bound to represent only one aspect of a complex set of issues.

Perhaps the very reason that day care has become such a hotly debated subject is that this service is viewed as a "solution" to a number of different problems, by several distinct and disparate groups. Expanding day care, through public subsidy, is said to be the key to getting people off welfare rolls, to liberating women, and to protecting children and stimulating their development. But the advocacy for public support of day care services, by the various different camps, yields no consensus about what these services should do, in terms of the care and development of children, what they should cost, to whom they should be made available, who should supply them, and how they should be administered and controlled.

It is to these kinds of questions that this volume is addressed. First, we hope our analysis will help to clarify some basic issues about public support for day care: what should be the rationale for such support, and what are the implications of this rationale for subsidy levels, quality standards, and eligibility policy. Our discussion is *not* a benefit/cost analysis of expanded day care, but an attempt to define the basis upon which subsidies, standards, and eligibility policies ought to be set.

The second and perhaps most important aspect of our discussion pertains to the organization of day care as an economic activity. It is our belief that even a well-formulated policy of public support for day care will be ineffective without the proper organizational machinery or "delivery system" to carry it out. Our discussion of organization begins with a review of how the delivery system is currently organized and what the problems are with present arrangements. This involves consideration of the fragmented structure of the federal grants apparatus affecting day care, problems of administration and regulation at the local level, and other factors which now hinder the quantity and quality of supply.

Next, we consider how the delivery system for day care ought to be structured if it is to be both responsive to demand and responsible in the quality of services it provides. Here we delve into questions of public, nonprofit, and profitmaking supplying agents, and various mechanisms for evaluating and controlling the performance of the local day care sector as a whole. This leads us to consider how day care can be planned and coordinated at the community level and what analytical tools may be used for this purpose.

We believe that our discussion should be of interest to several different audiences. Our analyses of both the rationale for public support and the organization of day care, have direct application to policymakers and governmental officials. The last chapter of this book is specifically addressed to national day care policy, and for good reasons. Several major pieces of new legislation affecting day care, emphasizing both welfare reform and child development, have recently come before Congress. We focus on one piece of legislation in particular, the Comprehensive Child Development Act, which was vetoed by the president in 1971 and has since been modified in Congress, but is nonetheless the most significant piece of day care legislation yet considered. We review both the content and the merits of this legislation, and how it might be changed and, in the event of its passage, followed up by federal, state, and local administrators. Of further interest to governmental officials should be our consideration of the present delivery system, which would not be entirely replaced by major new legislation, and which, in the absence of such legislation, might still be modified and molded into a more coordinated and consistent public day care system.

Finally, this book is addressed to the wide spectrum of interested citizens who are concerned with day care policy from various other points of view. Though we hope it will be read by analysts and scholars, this book is not a technical manual, or an esoteric theoretical analysis. It can be read by the interested layman as well as the expert. Our discussion is offered in the hope that it will be thoughtfully considered. The authors feel that there are some important things worth saying about day care policy and practice, and we have tried to say them. We will feel successful if people begin to discuss some of the issues in the way that we have posed them, rather than on the less satisfactory bases now often employed.

We hasten to add that the authors' competences are confined to economic and organizational matters; yet our discussion of necessity involves certain assumptions and implications regarding child development. Hence, we would welcome comments from scholars in other disciplines such as child psychology and education, where we claim no expertise. Within the limits of our understanding, we only wish to note that more research on the developmental benefits of programs for preschool children seems warranted.

A word on the style and organization of this book is appropriate. This volume is based on several separate pieces of research by the contributors, done originally for other purposes, in partial awareness of the work of each other. The original materials have been drawn together and rewritten to provide a cohesive statement on day care policy, organization, and planning. The material is presented in several different modes, including empirical documentation of day care programs and activities, conceptual analyses of issues, and illustration of methodology for planning and evaluation. Chapter 1, the introduction by Dennis Young and Emma Jackson, presents a brief history and sets forth the current policy issues surrounding extra-family day care in the United States. Chapter 2, by Richard Nelson and Michael Krashinsky, presents background on the sources and trends in the demand and supply of day care. Chapter 3, by Emma Jackson, documents and discusses the present system of publicly supported day care. Chapter 4 by Nelson and Krashinsky, is a normative analysis of public subsidy and organization of the day care sector, which develops in general terms what we think a desirable public policy would be. Chapter 5 by Richard Zamoff and Jerolyn Lyle, discusses the role of planning and evaluation in the organization and provision of local day care, and illustrates the use of a methodology for carrying out these functions. Finally, Chapter 6, by Richard Nelson and Dennis Young, summarizes the implications of our discussion in the context of national day care policy.

Acknowledgments

The authors would like to thank their colleagues at the Urban Institute—Harold Hochman and Worth Bateman for encouragement and editorial suggestions on this work, Cathy Gilson for helpful comments on various versions of the manuscript, and Marjorie Lissy for fact-finding in bringing parts of the manuscript up to date. The authors would also like to express special appreciation to several reviewers of the manuscript for their sharp-eyed criticisms and constructive suggestions, particularly Gwen Morgan, Senior Child Care Consultant, Office of State Planning and Management, Commonwealth of Massachusetts; also, Alice Rivlin, The Brookings Institution; Edward Gramlich, Office of Economic Opportunity; Joseph Wholey, The Urban Institute; and Ellen Brachman of the Division of Child Development, D.C. Department of Human Resources. Numerous other people are to be acknowledged for their assistance in the primary research efforts from which this volume has drawn its material. Many thanks are due the secretarial staff of the Urban Public Finance Group of The Urban Institute for yeoman work in typing several drafts. The authors assume full responsibility for any errors or inaccuracies. The work in this volume has been supported by the National Science Foundation and the Ford Foundation.

Public Policy for Day Care
of Young Children

1

Introduction

Dennis Young and Emma Jackson

The subject of this book is a service commonly called extra-family day care or just day care. The terms refer to full or part-time care for young (preschool) children outside their homes on a regular basis during the day, while their parents work or are engaged in other activities which separate them from their children. Day care currently takes place in a variety of environments including the homes of relatives or neighbors (where money payments may or may not be involved), in licensed or unlicensed private family day care homes run on a small scale by neighborhood residents, and formal day care centers and nursery schools. In this book, we use the terms extra-family day care, or day care, in connection with the more *formal* arrangements—day care centers and nursery schools, and to some extent licensed family day care homes. For these categories of day care supply are the ones principally at issue with respect to questions of public regulation and subsidy, and organization of the delivery system for day care.

While extra-family day care has recently become a subject of intense current interest and importance in the United States, this service has long been a part of this country's history and traditions. Extra-family day care has served many important functions in U.S. economic and social life including custody of children of working parents, early childhood education, and acculturation of immigrant children.

Historical records for day care in America date back to the mid-nineteenth century. In the custodial tradition, space was made available for the children of working mothers at the Nursery and Child's Hospital in New York City in 1854. The example was followed by the Virginia Nursery in 1872 and the Bethany Day Nursery in 1887. Offered for philanthropic assistance, these early

This chapter is based in part on Emma Jackson, "An Analysis of the Delivery of Day Care Services," Urban Institute Working Paper 1205-4, February 1972.

1

services were called day nurseries, and were designed to care for the child's physical needs while the parents were at work outside the home. While the child's intellectual, social, and emotional needs were not ignored, the basic (custodial) objective was fulfilled if the child had been fed, sheltered, protected from environmental hazards, and engaged in organized or free play activities at some time during the day.

Preschool education, on the other hand, developed historically within a middle-class context. The parent cooperative nursery movement of the 1920s, the university-based programs in home economics and psychology, and renewed interest in the Montessori movement of the 1960s all drew children from educated, articulate parents who shared many common assumptions with teachers about child growth and development. Preschool education focused on meeting the child's developmental needs: his verbal concepts and abilities, his interpersonal and social skills, and appreciation of learning.

While conveniently separated for purposes of our discussion, the custodial and educational traditions had much in common. The day nurseries were established by the first of this country's social welfare philanthropists, and were intended in part to instill cultural values in the children of the poor. There was more than a custodial agenda in the early day nurseries, and as they evolved they were influenced by the early childhood education movement. On the other hand, the first nursery *schools* shared with the day nurseries the objective of working with poor children in need of daily supervision, whose parents were employed in factories.[1]

Historically, federal support of day care services has reflected national emergencies and socioeconomic exigencies. The federal government provided major support for day care during the Civil War, World War I, the depression, and World War II. The trends of the times determined the criteria, the goals, the availability and costs of services, and the auspices under which services were provided. During the depression, for example, day care for children was financed by the federal government under the Federal Emergency Relief Administration and WPA. The primary objectives were to care for children of the economically deprived, and to provide employment to needy teachers, nurses, and social workers, janitors and cooks, as part of the work relief program engineered to counter unemployment.

As the 40s approached and WPA was no longer necessary as a source of employment, day care programs were phased out. But with World War II, the nation's males were drafted into the armed services, and women were called into the labor force:

> ... women were called into factories, and families by the thousands crowded into the war production areas. Children were being left alone, locked into parked cars, or forced to join the increasing numbers of "latchkey" children shifting for themselves.[2]

The day care sector expanded rapidly during the war, but again receded as the national emergency subsided.

The 1960s ushered in another period of federal involvement in day care, stimulated by national interest in questions of poverty and equal opportunity. Plans for reducing welfare rolls by getting mothers to work and providing day care for their children, were proposed during this period. Public emphasis on the preschool education tradition emerged for the first time, as research began to show that children from economically deprived environments started school developmentally behind their peers.[3] Provision of day care and preschool programs was advocated for the purpose of breaking the poverty cycle through early intervention in the child's life. The goal was to permit economically disadvantaged children to start school with similar experiential and intellectual equipment as children from more advantaged homes.[4]

In the early 1970s the debate over day care still reflects this service's mixed origins and sources of demand. The custodial function which day care serves is now emphasized not so much for reasons of war production or public employment, but for what we may term "the three w's"—working mothers, women's liberation, and welfare. The expanding role of women in the labor force, resulting from basic demographic and technological changes affecting the economy (as we discuss in Chapter 2), has increased the private economic demand for child care services. Work opportunities for women have expanded, and more women have found it economically necessary or worthwhile to take employment outside the home, and utilize day care services for their children. For many of these women the day care they can afford in the private marketplace is marginal in quality, or at least less attractive than they would like. Other women who would like to work are discouraged from doing so by the quality of day care they can afford. Such dissatisfaction with present day care arrangements has increased the demand for public support.

Parallel to the changes in the woman's role in the economy are changes in her social and political status that reflect a desire to participate in the world of commerce and government on an equal basis with men, and consequently to assume a less comprehensive responsibility for child care. The reduced availability of mothers' time devoted to child care would be made up by greater assumption of child care duties by men, and greater usage of extra-family day care. Thus, one plank in the women's lib platform is increased public support of day care.

A third source of support for the concept of day care in its custodial function arises out of the current furor over the nation's system of welfare. Some partisans to that debate emphasize the concept of "self-sufficiency" and the belief that all "able-bodied" welfare recipients should be required to work. Thus, training programs such as the WIN program, or welfare proposals such as the President's Family Assistance Plan include child care provisions. While one may question the economic rationale of requiring women to take low paying jobs while their children must be placed in either expensive or low quality day care programs, the welfare issue remains a major source of initiative for expansion of day care programs.

In the public policy discussion of child care centered on the "three w's," day care is an instrument to be used in achieving objectives defined in terms of benefits for adults. There has been a parallel discussion of day care rooted more directly in objectives defined in terms of benefits for children. The Comprehensive Child Care Act vetoed by President Nixon in 1971, and emerging in different versions in the Congress thereafter, stresses the educational and developmental rather than the purely custodial function of extra-family day care. It emphasizes the view that the principal reason for public support of day care should be to ensure that, for whatever economic or social reasons parents place their children in day care programs, the children will receive satisfactory care.

So many different strands of public interest and concern have not led to a unified political coalition for governmental support of day care. In fact, the different interest groups have competed with one another to influence public policy with the result that governmental jurisdiction over day care-related programs is fragmented and spread over a multiplicity of agencies at the national, state, and local levels. In essence, the diversity of interests has hindered the formulation of a coherent public day care policy.

It is essential, therefore, to step back from the individual perspectives of particular interest groups to consider what the goals of a public day care policy ought to be. Clearly, there are a number of related program goals such as employment, training, and reduction of welfare dependency whose pursuit increases the demand for extra-family day care in its custodial role. Making day care less expensive, more attractive, or more widely available will facilitate participation in activities which require day care as an adjunct. Thus proponents of training, employment, or welfare programs promote day care if lack of such services proves to be a roadblock to participation in their programs. In this sense, day care is similar to commuter transportation or conveniently located housing in the eyes of firms trying to hire employees. Housing and transportation are not the concern of such firms unless these functions are not properly taken care of elsewhere, and even then the concern is indirect, through salary considerations usually.

So it is for day care, which is a prerequisite to several (adult-related) social goals, but not the explicit responsibility of agencies concerned with those goals. Day care is primarily a service to children, and must be the explicit focus of those concerned with children's interests. Thus, in formulating day care policy, the focus must be on children, within the context of demand created by other interests. Specifically, one must ask—what do we want day care to do for children, given the fact that day care services will be used by some parents and will not be used by others, for various social and economic reasons. In general terms, the answer must be—we want to maintain and improve the quality of care to children. This goal has two important aspects: Primarily day care must cope with the increasing demand for extra-family day care arrangements arising out of underlying economic and social trends, so that children will not experience deterioration in the care they receive when they are placed in day care environments; and secondarily, demand for extra-family day care arrangements might be stimulated in some circumstances where such arrangements would be clear improvements in the care children receive at home.

The problems involved in addressing this goal derive from conditions on both the demand and supply sides of the day care "market." For while the demand for extra-family day care increases, the current supply arrangements suffer from a number of deficiencies which cause some of the care now provided to be of poor quality and thwart expansion of good quality services in response to demand increases. The mandate for public policy is to deal with these problems by manipulating two sets of interrelated policy variables: those variables which determine the level and distribution of public and private resources devoted to extra-family day care services, and those variables which determine how effectively those resources are used to deliver the desired services. The first category of variables includes the subsidy rates, fee schedules, quality standards, and eligibility guidelines for publicly supported day care. The second category involves the structure of the delivery system, including the economic nature of day care suppliers and the administrative and regulatory arrangements for coordinating and controlling the supply of services.

A number of fairly subtle points must be considered in determining how variables in the first category—the quality standards, eligibility policy, fees and subsidy schedules—should be set. Expanding the supply of good quality extra-family day care to serve growing demands, and to upgrade the quality of some of the care that is currently supplied, may require a major national commitment of public funds. But before the necessary level of support can be estimated, the question of what constitutes an acceptable quality of care must be agreed upon and its costs determined, the eligibility for such care must be specified, and the demand for such care must be calculated under proposed schedules of fees and subsidies. These determinations will set the basic tone for a publicly supported regime of day care services.

We will argue in this book that these elements of policy should be designed to make satisfactory day care services widely available to all children whose parents, for whatever private economic or social policy reasons, choose to or find it necessary to utilize extra-family day care arrangements. To preview our discussion, such policy would involve universal eligibility for all children, independent of their parents employment or training status; fees and subsidies keyed to family income to neutralize income barriers to the use of good quality care; and setting standards and subsidy rates at levels that will allow widely available care of "good" quality, rather than "very expensive" care limited to a few.

Within the basic framework of standards, eligibility, and subsidy policy, the effective quality, efficiency, and availability of day care services will be greatly influenced by the way the delivery system for day care is organized. Here, the two primary issues are: how can day care services be regulated to ensure that desired quality is maintained; and how can the supply be coordinated and stimulated to serve changing demands in an efficient and responsive manner. Again, to preview our discussion, our view is that for quality to be assured, day care programs must operate in a "fishbowl environment" of parental overview and participation in policymaking. Parents must also have a choice of programs to patronize. These requirements seem best fulfilled by a regime in which individual suppliers are responsible to parent-oriented councils, and paid and subsidized according to the enrollments they attract. The requirement of parental overview and participation would seem to favor the nonprofit form of supply agency, but does not rule out participation of profitmaking firms that wish to comply with the "fishbowl" specifications. Indeed, maintaining at least a fringe of private profitmaking day care providers seems highly useful for facilitating supply adjustment through the conventional incentives of the marketplace.

But our analysis of supply questions also indicates the need for an additional delivery system component—a central community planning and coordinating agency to stimulate and channel the supply of services to match demand. For in the context of a day care sector in which a large part of the supply is not especially motivated by profits, consumers may not be made aware of the available options, and suppliers may not be informed of the outstanding demands for day care. In addition, the fact that nonprofit-oriented suppliers may be weakly motivated to respond to outstanding demands suggests a need for a central agency capable of encouraging new ventures and bringing the financial and legal prerequisites to bear on this objective. In order to carry out its mission such an agency will require control over public funds. But equally as important the community agency must have analytical capability to plan and evaluate local day care needs and performance, based on systematic information. Part of our discussion here documents evaluation methodology that may be used for this purpose.

In summary, the basic elements of public support and the organization of the delivery system for extra-family day care are what we address here. Our intent is to suggest a constructive approach to establishing a vital, reliable, and smoothly functioning day care sector at a time when national policy for day care is under debate, and local day care is in disarray. But while the issues are difficult to resolve, the rewards for satisfactory resolution are great. For what is done in the next few years will probably determine the direction and performance of day care services for many years to come, and the fortunes of many young children as a result.

2

The Demand and Supply of Extra-Family Day Care

Richard Nelson and Michael Krashinsky

Introduction

One argument often heard in the recent debate is that extra-family day care is "unnatural" and damaging to family structure. Certainly this is the flavor of President Nixon's 1971 veto message regarding the child development legislation.[1] Most young children are cared for by their parents, and the American attitude seems to be that this is the appropriate way to get that job done, except where welfare recipients are involved. However, a central thrust of this chapter is that the rising demand for extra-family day care of children is in good part the result of basic demographic and technological changes which make it increasingly sensible and efficient to care for a growing number of our young children outside of the traditional family context.

Another argument often raised against public expenditure for day care is that the cost of extra-family care is inordinately high. While this objection ignores the unpriced resources which are spent on child care within the family, the concern over costs is easy to understand. In 1970 there were roughly eighteen million American children under five years of age. Existing standards for day care funded under federal programs require a minimum of one adult for every five young children, or more than three and one-half million adults required for day care, roughly double the number of teachers presently in our public schools. Even at the ratio of one adult to eight children (about the average for day care centers in 1970), an average salary of $4,000 per year per day care worker (again about average) and total costs about 1.3 times salary cost, the bill in 1970 would have been roughly $13 billion a year for providing full day care to all children under five.[2] This is why many people boggle at

This chapter is based on Richard R. Nelson and Michael Krashinsky, "Some Questions of Optimal Organization: The Case of Day Care for Children," Urban Institute Working Paper 1205-2, December 1971.

the notion of establishing a national system of extra-family day care, although the cost per child for a year in the above calculation is only $650, less than one-third what the Office of Child Development believes is necessary for a desirable level of care.

Such an expenditure calculation assumes that all children under five would participate in full day care. But even under a regime of fully subsidized "free" day care, many children would continue to be cared for at home, or in other less comprehensive arrangements. Not all parents want full day care, or any day care, for their children. Nevertheless, a substantial fraction of young children would probably use such services, hence a program of universal free day care would involve a very large outlay of public funds.

However, the argument about high cost neglects consideration of unpaid resources. Whether or not the nation establishes a system of institutions to provide day care, employs people to operate them, and has the cost reflected in a monetary total, many million of adults will be engaged in day care activities. Most of this activity is undertaken within the family. The fact that, usually, no money passes hands in quid pro quo means that this activity does not show up in the GNP accounts. But the resources involved are no less real because of this. The provision of specialized day care facilities for children presently cared for at home would involve a change in mechanism, but it is *not* clear that it would involve a major increase in resources actually allocated to day care. Children must be cared for wherever they are located. Indeed, one of the arguments *for* specialized extra-family day care is that it might reduce the resources applied, through various economies of scale and specialization. This fact, in part, explains why many families purchase day care for their children even in the absence of subsidy.

Demand for Extra-Family Day Care

The private component of demand can be defined as the outside care families are willing to pay for out of their own pockets. Private demand for day care depends on a number of variables, including the number and ages of the children and the number and status of the adults in the family. It depends on what the adults can earn outside the home with time freed by day care, on what can be earned at home along with child care, and on the cost of day care. It depends on the preferences of family adults regarding employment or, more generally, the time freed from child care, beliefs about the benefits or penalties to their children associated with various forms of child care, and on the wealth of the family, which determines the extent to which preferences can be indulged.

It would appear that demographic, economic, and attitudinal trends all have worked in the direction of increasing demand for extra family day care. The decline in mortality rates, both for children and adults, has resulted in quite remarkable changes over the years in the characteristics of the American family. Schultz, among others, has argued that the pattern of birth can be explained largely by the number of surviving children the parents deem appropriate and the regime of child mortality.[3] While it seems a good bet that there has been a significant long-run decline in average family goals regarding the number of surviving children, there is no hard evidence on this. Given a constant or a falling family-size goal, the decline in child death rates experienced over the last half century would have led to a decline in the number of desired births and young children per family (because of higher survival rates). The mortality declines have been dramatic. In 1900, mortality for children under one year was 162 per thousand. It was over 50 per thousand in 1940. Since the late 1950s is has tended to be under 30 per thousand. The death rate declines for young children have been almost as dramatic. The death rate for children one to four years has fallen from 19 per thousand in 1900, to 2.9 in 1949, to about 1.1 in the late 1950s where it has stabilized. Birth rates have adjusted in compensation. The results of these trends have been a significant, if somewhat erratic, long-run decline in the number of children under five per woman in the twenty to forty-four years old age range. The figure was 1.3 in 1800. The ratio was in the neighborhood of .7 or .8 in 1900, declined to .4 in 1940, increased in the postwar years, and fell to .35 in 1970.[4]

Corresponding to changes in birth rates, the median age of women at the birth of the last child has declined from the late thirties around 1800 to the early thirties in 1900 to the late twenties today. Over the same period the life expectancy of women at age twenty has risen by twenty years, ten since 1900. With a decline in the age where childbearing (childrearing) is complete and an increase in life expectancy a significant number of years remain on average to a woman after her childrearing tasks have become minimal, something that was not true during the early 1800s and far from the rule in the early twentieth century.[5]

These demographic developments have strengthened the economic rationale for extra-family day care. For families with three or more young children the economies of extra-family day care are questionable. If the children stay at home with the mother she is pretty well occupied with their care and other activities around the home. If she sends them to a day care center, while she is relieved, someone else is required to do a comparable amount of work. Standards for federally funded day care require that the adult/child ratio shall not be diluted below 1 to 5 for very young children. In the day care centers examined by the Westinghouse survey, the average adult/child ratio was less than this, roughly 1 in 8.[6] But other costs are also involved in specialized day care. While home space can be used for in-home day care, special facilities may be needed for care outside the home. For families with one or two young children, however, the effort associated with their care at a day care center would appear small compared to the mother's time freed. A trend toward families with a smaller number of children, then, should increase the efficiency of specialized day care relative to care within the core family.[7]

The increase in the number of years left to a woman after child care responsibilities have become minimal has also worked in this direction. With a longer expected potential working life various sorts of investment in future earning power become sensible. Completing college, or taking graduate work or professional training, which might not be a good investment if time horizons are short, may become an excellent investment when time horizons are longer, and paying the price in terms of day care may then be an attractive proposition.

Not only demographic but economic developments, especially the shift of productive employment outside the home, have acted to increase the demand for day care. Not more than a century ago many families took care of a large fraction of their needs through their home activities. Even specialized activities, like cash crop farming or blacksmithing, often took place at or close to the home. But the steady and accumulatively vast increases in productivity in specialized economic institutions outside the home have led to the demise of the family as a general purpose economic organization. Clothes, for example, which used to be manufactured at home are now far more efficiently produced by commercial firms. The result is that one or more members of the family had to leave the home to find employment and earn a salary, if family income was to keep pace with rising productivity. Usually, the man of the house would do so, but the same factors that caused men to leave their homes for work apply to women as well. Improved technology in the home, for cooking and cleaning and so on, and the shift of other activities such as clothes manufacture and food preparation away from the home, meant that women could fulfill their remaining household responsibilities and still hold down outside employment. And these same economic developments meant that if women were to have a cash income or a productive career they had to leave the daytime household.

But coupled with the increased economic imperatives for men and women to seek employment outside the home were parallel developments which made intrafamily child care less accessible. As men left their families for the working day their by-product, child-watching capabilities have been lost. In addition, technical advance and increasing urbanization tended to break up extended families as grown up children moved away from the rural environment to find better jobs. Hence, grandmothers or other relatives became less available for child care duties. Thus today, much more than years ago, there is a sharp tension between the mother's motivation to work and her desire to have her children cared for within a family context. The decision of the mother to work outside the family now often requires use of extra-family day care arrangements for her young children.

The demographic and economic factors that have increased the value of the mother's time free from child care responsibilities have certainly been the principle causes of the rise in work force participation among married women, from 5 percent in 1890 to 30 percent in 1960 to 40 percent in 1970. Participation rates for women with children under six increased from 12 percent in 1950 to 19 percent in 1960 to 28 percent in 1969.[8] This great increase probably overstates what has happened. In 1890 almost certainly a larger fraction of married women worked on the family farm or along with their husbands; this is not adequately reflected in the 5 percent figure. However, in all likelihood the increase has been dramatic.

For families where there is only one parent in the house or where a single salary yields an inadequate living, in the absence of income support from outside the family, there is no real choice. The mother must work for a money income, and as a rule this means she must work outside the home. Thus it is not surprising that a considerable fraction of the demand for day care is from female-headed families, with black urban families more than proportionately represented in this group. The increase in the percentage of families that are headed by females has attracted much attention as a factor behind rising demands for day care. This development is in part independent of, in part the result of, the trends towards urbanization and family specialization discussed above. What is seldom recognized is that in the absence of these trends single-adult nuclear families would be far better able to cope without extra-family day care. Opportunities to meet needs by household work, either directly or for money, would be greater. Extended-family child care assistance would be more available. The structure of the modern urban economy results in a particularly severe economic dilemma for poor or female-headed urban families with young children.

For two-parent families in which the earning potential of the husband approaches the national average, there certainly is a choice of whether the wife works and extra-family day care is used. Thus, it is more difficult to assess the strength of private demand for extra-family day care for these families. Certainly a family in which the husband earns an adequate income has an increased ability to follow its preferences and pay less attention to the strictly financial aspects of a choice. While for families with two able-bodied parents and a small number of children it may be more efficient for the mother to choose a career and put her children in day care, if the single salary is adequate there is no imperative to do this. Mincer's study shows a decreasing participation rate for wives as the husband's salary increases, even after correcting for the effects of the wife's earning potential and education.[9] The decision of middle- and high-income intact families to use day care for the children can hinge largely on the attitudes of a wife toward a career and her beliefs about what is best for the children. These attitudes clearly are related to her level of education. Well-educated wives have higher work participation rates than women with lower levels of educational attainment. (However there also is evidence that of the mothers of very young children, those mothers with higher education tend to have a lower work force participation rate than those with less education.) It is difficult to disentangle cause from effect. Both higher educational levels and greater work force participation reflect, and have caused, significant changes in attitudes toward careers for women. Among middle- and upper-income Americans the sharp rise of children in nursery school also may be as much a result of beliefs that this is good for children as it is a result of the economic attractiveness of day care. Again it is impossible to disentangle motives completely. But in any case, the wife following a career because she finds it personally as well as financially rewarding, and children in nursery school because it is believed they enjoy it and benefit from it, certainly is a growing pattern among middle- and upper-class Americans.

The demand for day care is, of course, not strictly private. Almost all societies have expressed concern and taken some responsibility for the care and upbringing of young children, and child care never has been purely a family matter. Social intervention in child care has been motivated in part by concern for children as people who, in the absence of parental resources or appropriate attitudes, are in need of public protection. Orphanages and like institutions long have been publicly provided. The public long has intervened in instances of brutality of parents towards children. A good part of the social legislation of the last 150 years has been concerned with protecting children from their parents' and employers' exploitation. Social intervention also has been motivated by the understanding that our children of today will be tomorrow's adults, and that rearing children is society's most important investment in the future. Public provision of funds for education and laws that make education compulsory are perhaps the most common manifestation of this investment motive.

As noted earlier, there has been a long if erratic public involvement in the day care of preschool-age children motivated by all of these societal concerns. Under Settlement House and other auspices, day care has been provided for children of poor families where the only parent or both parents had to work. During the heavy wave of immigration day care nurseries were viewed by a number of Americans as a vehicle for acculturating children of (poor) immigrants. And, day care traditionally has been a form of assistance and treatment for troubled families advocated by social workers.[10]

Since 1960 there has been a significant increase in federal funding and public support of day care.[11] The content of funding legislation is discussed in the next chapter. These public funds have added to private resources, in generating growing day care demand.

The Supply of Extra-Family Day Care

What kind of supply has private and public demand and money brought forth to date? The (extended) family is still the most important source of supply of care for young children whose mothers are working or otherwise absent. Of the children of full- and part-time working mothers sampled in the Low and Spindler study, 80 percent were cared for by someone in the family. For children of full-time working mothers the figure was 53 percent.[12] These figures presumably include both care provided in the children's homes and care provided in the relatives' homes. The Zamoff and Vogt study of day care in the Washington, D.C., Model Neighborhood shows that 67 percent of the children of working mothers (full or part time) were cared for by a family member in the child's home, and 19 percent of the children were cared for by a relative in the relative's home.[13] No data were collected regarding money payments. Some money may have been involved, but it is quite clear that money payment is not the principal inducement in drawing forth the supply of extended-family child care. Rather, the principal inducement is the more diffuse bond of family empathy.

In 10 percent of the cases studied by Zamoff and Vogt in the Washington, D.C., Model Neighborhood, and in 23 percent of the cases studied by Zamoff and Lyle in the Mount Pleasant neighborhood,[14] the supplier was labeled a babysitter who either came to the child's house, or cared for the child in her own home. Zamoff's "sitter" category undoubtedly overlaps the "family day care home" category of the Westinghouse study. In the latter study roughly 850,000 children were found to be cared for in outside homes in which one or more sitters cared for one to six children. While these cases may involve elements of neighborliness and service to local children, the inducement of money payment is also very important.

These mechanisms—supply of other family help, and small-scale private enterprise—account for the lion's share of day care not provided by the mother in both the Low and Spindler and the Zamoff studies. These arrangements, largely conducted in someone's existing house, avoid the need to build extra facilities. Their prevalence also suggests that economies of scale in child care are realized rather quickly, that is, that the major efficiency gains come from having one adult supervise five or six children rather than one or two.

In good part induced by the availability of public funds, there has been a rapid expansion over the last decade in large-scale licensed day care centers. Steiner reports that the number of licensed centers increased from 4,400 in 1960 to 13,600 in 1969. (However, it is hard to separate increases in the number of day care centers from increased licensing of preexisting centers and family day care homes. Many state licensing laws were passed in the period 1960-62.)[15] The Westinghouse study has provided a wealth of detail on the current situation regarding licensed centers, i.e., licensed facilities providing care to groups of seven or more children with full-time care available (the latter characteristic ruling out, for example, many nursery schools and many Headstart centers). An estimated 17,500 centers of this sort existed in 1970, caring for approximately 575,000 children on a full-day basis and additional children part time. (The discrepancies from the numbers reported by Steiner are the result of differences in both definition and estimation procedures.) The costs of full-time child care per month in these centers range from about $40 in centers that provided "custodial" care without a structured educational program, to about $60 a month for a center that provided a "minimal" educational program, to over $200 a month in some centers that provided a "rich" educational program, medical care, consulting services to both children and parents, etc. (Note that these numbers apply to the late 1960s; prices have risen significantly since that time.)

The bulk of these expenses were personnel costs. The estimated staff of the centers consisted of 7,500 full-time workers, and 5,100 part-timers. By and large, day care workers had no special education or training. Most teachers and directors did not have college degrees. The median reported income for full-time workers was only $350 a month. Average equipment per child averaged approximately $100. Presumably this does not include the costs of the building. Unlike the informal arrangements, day care centers tend to use special facilities. Approximately 50 percent of the centers in the sample had their own building. Most of the rest undoubtedly occupied space that had alternative uses and costs. Centers varied greatly in both staffing and in equipment and facilities.

By way of caution to the reader, although the Westinghouse study is a major source of comprehensive data on day care, clearly the cost figures must not be taken too literally. In particular, one must be wary of comparing "costs" of surveyed centers whose quality and budgeting procedures may differ. Classifying centers by broad "custodial" or "developmental" categories, in order to correct for quality differences, fails to penetrate what is really going on in a center and how competently care is provided. Further, the presence of non-monetized resource inputs such as volunteer labor or rent-free space in a church or other such facility, must be corrected for if costs figures are to be made comparable among different centers. In addition, budgeting of ancillary services such as medical or dental care must be separated from the budgeting of day care expenditures per se in comparing budgets of different centers, and normalizing for quality differences.[16]

Sixty percent of the centers in the Westinghouse study were proprietary, and these cared for about half of the day care children. Almost all of the income of these centers came from fees paid by the parents, although these fees themselves sometimes were partially underwritten by public assistance. Proprietary centers accounted for the bulk of the custodial and "lean educational" centers but also for some of the fancier ones.

Most of the rest were nonproprietary centers; a small fraction were government operated. Churches provided facilities for 18 percent of the children. Many facilities were associated with community action agencies. A few were run by public schools or state welfare departments. A few (not reported in the Westinghouse study) are associated with places of work.

The Westinghouse study suggests that the nonproprietary centers, as the proprietary ones, span the spectrum of (budgeted) day care costs. However, the nonproprietary centers account for a larger fraction of the expensive centers than they do the less expensive centers. A far smaller fraction of the cost of the nonproprietary centers, as compared with the proprietary ones, came from parents' fees. Parents' fees in the high-cost centers operated by nonprofit or public organizations did not tend to be much higher than fees in the low-cost proprietary centers, on the average about $40 per child per month. The higher costs were covered by philanthropy or public subsidy under a wide range of governmental programs.

Public subsidy has been a principal force in creating a formal and informal regulatory and planning superstructure on top of the institutions directly providing day care services. Part of public subsidy is channeled through welfare agencies, part through community action agencies, model cities, and other organizations. The provision of public funds to largely nongovernmental day care centers has required, in the eyes of Congress, that certain day care standards be met. It also has generated legal requirements for mechanisms of overall planning and coordination of day care in a neighborhood, city, or region. Reflecting the spirit of the times, federal requirements have established the principle, if not necessarily the fact, of active community and parental participation in these activities.

However, it is interesting that for all the discussion of public provision of day care, the vast bulk of child care arrangements made for extra-family care were hardly touched by public policy, much less subsidy. The number of day care slots totally or partially supported through federal funds certainly is less than 10 percent of the number of children under five with working mothers. The principal effect of federal money has been to subsidize a small portion of total day care arrangements, permitting these to offer more expensive care for children of poor families, charging the families nothing or no more than the less resource-intensive modes of care. But the bulk of extra-family child care apparently has been untouched by federal programs.

Similarly, the bulk of extra-family child care is unaffected by the regulatory process. Significantly, less than 10 percent of the family day care *homes* sampled in the Westinghouse study were licensed or regulated in some way. The day care centers were much more under (nominal) licensing and regulatory control. Ninety percent of the centers sampled by Westinghouse were licensed, which meant that they were subject to minimum standards of space, cleanliness, staffing, and program enforceable under the police powers of state and local government. In addition, centers receiving federal subsidy were subject to standards imposed by individual federal programs as well as Federal Interagency Day Care Requirements (see Chapter 3); these represent the level of quality (program and staff) that the federal government is presumed willing to support, and which may be enforced by cutting off funds. However, many of these regulatory requirements were nominal rather than real. Most states have given little support to staffing licensing agencies, while the federal government has failed to establish any monitoring system for enforcing its requirements for funding.

In summary, public support or regulation currently affects only a small fraction of children in day care. But rising private demand and public clamor for day care programs, and concern for their quality, could change this. If the magnitude of public subsidy does increase substantially over the next decade, such an increase would hopefully be accompanied by closer scrutiny of present governmental machinery for regulating day care and allocating day care resources.

3

The Present System of Publicly Supported Day Care

Emma Jackson

Introduction

Federal support for day care has risen from less than ten million dollars in the early 1960s to 332 million dollars, affecting 668,000 children, in 1971,[1] exclusive of income tax deductions for day care now permitted under the Internal Revenue Act of 1971. The growth of public support for day care has been accompanied by a proliferation of many different federal programs.

However, as this book goes to press, major changes are being made in the concept of federal support for delivery of public services, and these may render parts of the discussion in this chapter obsolete. In particular, present federal programs are being dismantled in favor of special and general revenue sharing to states and localities. The potential long-run impact of this policy on day care is beyond the scope of our discussion here. We only note that the revenue-sharing concept bears both risks and potential for improved day care services. Much will depend on the sensitivities and capabilities of state and local governments to address child care needs, and the extent to which the federal government replaces withdrawn grants-in-aid monies with revenue-sharing funds.

Federal Preschool and Day Care Programs, 1971[2]

The bulk of funds, covering the great majority of young children for which federal day care subsidies are provided, fall under the programs discussed below. The nature and funding of these programs are displayed in Table 3-1. (However, the expenditure figures should be viewed with some caution, as the sources of data are of limited

This chapter is based on Emma Jackson, "An Analysis of the Delivery of Day Care Services," Urban Institute Working Paper 1205-4, February 1972.

21

Table 3-1
Major Federal Preschool and Day Care Programs

	Social Security Act			Economic Opportunity Act		Elementary and Secondary Education Act
	AFDC Title IVA	WIN Title IVC	Child Welfare Services Title IVB	Headstart Title IIA Sect. 22 (a) 1	CEP Title IB Sect. 123 (A,B)	ESEA Title I Sect. 103 (a) 1
Day Care Expenditures for Fiscal Year 1971	130 million[a]	$26 million	$20 million[b]	$363 million	about $12 million[c]	$92 million
Federal Share	75%	90%[d]	Variable Match[e]	80%	90%	100%
Administrating Agency Federal	U.S. Dept. of Health, Education & Welfare Community Services Admin.			HEW, Office of Child Development	DOL Manpower Admin.	HEW, Office of Education
State Agency		Welfare Department			State Employment Service	State Dept. of Education
Local Agency		Welfare Department		CAP or Single Purpose Headstart Agency	CAP	Local Education Department
Eligible Operators[f]	1-8	1-8	1-7	1-5	1-5	1-9

aDoes not include $68 million Income Disregard for day care.

bUnofficial approximation.

cTotal CEP funding is approximately $170 million of which $158 is spent directly on training and work support.

dFormerly 75% until recent passage of the Talmadge Amendments; see text.

eVaries from state to state according to formula involving child population under 21 and state per capita income.

fEligible Operators Include:
  1. State Welfare Agency
  2. Local Welfare Agency
  3. Community Action Agency
  4. Neighborhood Organization
  5. Private Nonprofit Organizations
  6. Independent Operators
  7. Private Employers, Labor Unions
  8. Local Education Agency

Sources:

1. Patricia G. Bourne et al., "Day Care Nightmare," Working Paper No. 145, Institute of Urban and Regional Development, University of California at Berkeley, February 1971, Table I, p. 18.

2. *Federal Programs for Young Children* (Child Development Staff: Appalachian Region Commission, 1601 Connecticut Avenue, N.W., Washington, D.C.), October 1970.

3. *Special Analyses of the United States Government*, Fiscal Year 1973, and Fiscal Year 1972.

4. Private Communications, from officials at National Institutes of Education and D.C. Division of Child Development.

accuracy.) These programs, by and large, do not operate directly on supply, but rather supplement the demand for day care services generally provided through private, nonprofit auspices.

Social Security Act (as amended), 1967

Day care for children of welfare recipients has been part of the Social Security Act since 1962, but the 1967 amendments significantly broadened its authorization. This legislation includes some of the most important child care programs currently in operation.

Aid to Families With Dependent Children (AFDC) (Title IVA, Sec. 402(a) 14). This section of the Social Security Act enables state welfare departments to provide day care services to nearly all children from low-income families. Eligibility may be defined by states to include past, current, and potential welfare recipients. Under this section, the federal government (through the Department of Health, Education and Welfare) will match a state welfare department contribution on a 3 to 1 basis. Services may be provided directly by state or county welfare departments or may be contracted out to other government agencies or private organizations. Direct assistance to individuals is also authorized. More detail on the Title IVA (AFDC) program will be provided later.

Work Incentive Program (WIN) (Title IVC). Amendments in this section of the Social Security Act require states to mount an intensive effort to place all appropriate adult welfare recipients in jobs or in job training. The 1972 Talmadge amendments now require mothers of children over six years of age to register for work or training under WIN, as a prerequisite for AFDC welfare payments. By virtue of the latter amendments, the federal government now pays 90 percent of the cost for day care of children of WIN trainees; formerly it paid 75 percent. Funds are distributed by HEW to state and local welfare departments which may then operate programs, contract for services, or give direct assistance to individuals for privately arranged services.

Child Welfare Services (Title IVB. Sec. 422(a)). Under this section, grants from the federal government are authorized to state welfare agencies for child welfare services, including day care. Priority must be given to children from low-income families, and to those geographic areas with the greatest relative need for extension of day care services. The federal contribution varies from state to state according to the child population under twenty-one and the average per capita income. Direct assistance to individuals is not authorized under this section.

Economic Opportunity Act (as amended), 1964

Headstart (Title IIA, Sec. 222(a) 1). This section of the act is administered by the Office of Child Development in the Department of Health, Education and Welfare; it is a compensatory education program. Ninety percent of the children participating in any Headstart program must come from poor families. The stated purpose of the program is to improve the health and physical ability of poor children, to develop self-confidence, ability to relate to others, to increase perceptive skills, to involve parents in activities with children, and to provide appropriate social services for the family so that the poor child might begin his school career on more nearly equal terms with his more fortunate classmates. Funds (80 percent federal share) flow from HEW directly to local community action agencies which must provide 20 percent support, usually in kind. A community action agency may run programs directly or contract for services with public or private nonprofit agencies. State authority is limited to a simple approval or rejection process. Although $70 million of the original $425 million budget was allocated for day-long, full-year programs, the main thrust has been toward part-day compensatory education programs. New guidelines will take Headstart out of the full-day care business entirely.

Concentrated Employment Program (Title IB Sec. 123 (A,B)). This section represents an effort to provide a package of manpower programs in areas with serious unemployment problems. Day care may be provided for those enrolled in such a program. Funds are allocated by the Department of Labor, Manpower Administration, to selected state employment services and community action agencies; these are very limited in number.

Elementary and Secondary Education Act 1965

Title I of this act provides funds to school districts for projects designed to meet the needs of educationally deprived children from low-income families. Full financing (requiring no matching funds) is provided by the U.S. Office of Education to state departments of education for local distribution to school districts and other public agencies. The program requires districts to submit plans and applications to the state for expenditure of their federal entitlement. Compensatory preschool education programs for low-income children may be included in these plans. Title III of the act provides funds to school districts for model preschools.

Other Direct Funds

A host of other federal programs may provide funds for child care services or facilities. For example, Model Cities program funds may be channeled to Model Cities agencies, via mayors' offices, to directly fund child care or to be used as local matching funds in Title IVA grants. (About $9 million of Model Cities funds were used for day care in fiscal year 1971.) Urban Renewal monies may be utilized to acquire land; PHS Neighborhood Health Center funds may be used for construction which can include space for child care; neighborhood centers developed under the Economic Opportunity Act, or Community Health Centers under NIMH, may include child care provisions. Community Action Agency Program "packages" include preschool and child care services. HEW funds for Cuban immigrants and Department of the Interior funds for American Indians are also available for child care. Other sources include vocational education funds which high schools and community colleges may use for setting up laboratory preschools and day care centers, maternal and child health grants to states, Emergency Employment Act funds to support jobs in day care centers, Regional Commission funds for use in rural areas in the same way that Model Cities funds are used in urban areas, Neighborhood Youth Corps funds and Public Service Careers funds under the Economic Opportunity Act, JOBS funds under the Department of Labor to provide day care for enrollees of these programs, and Education Impact Aid funds.

A Closer Look at Title IVA (AFDC) of the Social Security Act

The federal grant apparatus for day care is complex not only in its multiplicity of different programs, but in the administrative structure of individual programs as well. Title IVA of the Social Security Act, an especially important component of the federal array of programs, may not be the most difficult to master. Yet it provides a good illustration of the kinds of requirements, procedures, and constraints for funding state and local agencies, that characterize federal grant programs for day care.

Recipient Eligibility

Under Title IVA, a state is allowed to provide day care services to past and potential AFDC recipients as well as those presently receiving assistance. Each state is free to identify and define "past and potential" recipients in its state plan under which it receives federal funding. Usually, a past recipient is a parent who, within a certain number of years, has been a welfare recipient. A potential recipient is a parent who is likely to become a recipient if the needed child welfare services (day care) are not provided. These recipients may fall into one of four categories:

1. Individuals who are medically needy.
2. Individuals who would qualify if the earnings exemption granted to recipients applied to them.
3. Those who are likely to receive financial assistance within five years.
4. Those who live in low-income neighborhoods at or near the dependency level.

Neighborhood Eligibility

Neighborhoods with a high rate of present, former, and potential recipients can be eligible for child care services. Any geographic area which meets the criteria of poverty established by the state agency, or any area approved for a federally-assisted antipoverty project, would be an appropriate neighborhood. When the neighborhood has been designated as impoverished and the street boundaries established, anyone (regardless of income) residing within the neighborhood becomes eligible for the service. The advantage of determining eligibility by neighborhood rather than by individuals is that the only criteria needed to establish a parent's eligibility is his address. This provides for great administrative simplicity and improved program morale associated with not having to discriminate among people in a given locale. No disclosure of income, marital status, etc., is necessary. The principal disadvantage is that poor people outside the neighborhood may not be able to receive the service while not so poor people within the area may be served. Frequently, if programs are not full to capacity, however, families outside of the neighborhood can apply on an individual basis.

States may also service geographic areas according to priority, and progressively expand the programs to other geographic areas where need is greatest. (Pending Title IVA guidelines may, however, eliminate geographic determination of eligibility in favor of individual determination.)

Administration and Regulations

The approval, interpretation, and ultimate authority for Title IVA grants rest with HEW's Social and Rehabilitation Service (SRS), but the programs are administered by a state agency (welfare department). For a state to receive these funds, the federal government must approve the state plan for administration of AFDC. The state welfare department then receives payments on a reimbursement basis from SRS (Public Assistance Unit). The state may provide day care services in various ways:

1. It may pay the cost of child care on an individual (child) basis in an existing program.
2. It may operate programs of its own where the day care personnel will be employed by the Welfare Department.
3. It may choose to subcontract with another agency or organization to operate a program.

Title IVA is a matching program under which the federal government provides 75 percent of the costs, with the 25 percent local matching share coming from state or local government, private funds donated by individuals, or from other sources such as the United Fund, foundation grants, Model Cities, religious and civic organizations, business, or labor. Until 1972 the Title IVA program was open-ended; the federal government would continue to match local funds in a 3 to 1 ratio, no matter how much was expended. In recent years a growing number of states began to take advantage of Title IVA and other open-ended provisions of the Social Security Act as general funding sources for financing social services. In fact, some states have used resources for existing (rather than new) services as matching funds to finance budget deficits, as if these grant programs were tantamount to general revenue sharing. Thus costs to the federal government have increased rapidly, from less than $1 billion in 1969 to $4.6 billion in 1972, for open-ended social services grants. However, in 1972 Congress voted, as part of federal revenue-sharing legislation, a $2.5 billion "lid" on these programs, coupled with a population-based formula to allocate appropriations among states. Thus, states such as California, Illinois, and New York, which took early advantage, and other states such as Maryland, which had planned to, now face severe problems in funding ongoing and planned day care services.[3]

Another stipulation of the Title IVA grant process is that private matching funds may not revert directly back to the donor agency. Thus, a private group that wishes to secure Title IVA assistance for the purpose of providing day care services through an organization affiliated with that group must (nominally) follow a rather involved process of raising the private matching funds, navigating them through an independent source (e.g., charity organization), which then must "donate" these funds to the state welfare department. The welfare department can then provide the full federal plus private shares to the applicant group. The foregoing process was designed to guard against coopting of public policy by large donors. A donor agency which relinquishes some of its charitable funds to the Welfare Department in order to bring in more federal dollars has no guarantee that those dollars will flow back again to itself. In practice, however, the provision seems to work against agencies struggling to provide services, not the donor agencies per se; the latter is pretty much assured that its money will be spent in the way it designates.

Title IVA is also subject to a requirement called "statewideness." Since 1935, Social Security laws have required that AFDC services be provided uniformly to every "political subdivision" in a state. This requirement is intended to prevent discrimination against any group or individual, and to assure that all who need services receive them. This principle of "statewideness" obliges a state to offer any service available to past, present, or potential AFDC recipients in the state who meet the criteria. If a group determination is made on the basis of a selected type of geographic area, coverage and service must be expanded to all similarly designated areas in the state. However, a recent interpretation of statewideness from SRS takes into consideration the needs and resources of the state. Now, in essence, a state need only provide evidence of a genuine commitment to provide services on a statewide basis within a reasonable time. The state must show that resources are or will be available to meet this commitment. Also, a certain level of service must be provided statewide, even in the early stages; for example, eligible recipients must be referred to existing services. The memorandum suggests that a state's willingness to take time and effort to determine areas of need in the state, nature of the needs, and extent of community involvement and participation, can be a useful measure of the state's commitment to statewideness.

 Coordination at the Federal Level

In 1968 the Federal Panel on Early Childhood was established by the Secretary of Health, Education and Welfare, at the request of the president, to coordinate and improve all early childhood programs financed by federal funds. The panel includes representatives of federal agencies concerned with services to families and children—HEW, the Departments of Labor, Agriculture, Commerce, Interior, Defense, and Housing and Urban Development, the Office of Economic Opportunity, and the Office of Management and Budget. Its purpose is to develop plans for the most effective use of child care funds for operation, research, training, and technical assistance available to each of the departments and agencies.

The Federal Interagency Day Care Requirements developed by the panel emphasize "more than custodial care, and devotion to vigorous young minds and bodies." The requirements apply to a variety of settings including:

1. Day Care Centers—more than five children, usually of preschool age.
2. Family Day Care Homes—less than five children of all ages cared for in a woman's home.
3. Group Day Care Homes—up to twelve children cared for in a woman's home.
4. In-Home Care—the caretaker comes into the child's own home.

Standards cover a range of subjects including environment, educational services, social services, health and nutrition services, training parent involvement, administration and evaluation.

In addition to standards, the Federal Panel on Early Childhood drew up a plan to coordinate all programs that provide services to children and their families. The program, called the Community Coordinated Child Care (4-C) Program, is administered by the Office of Child Development of HEW. It is an effort to achieve coordination of all day care-related organizations within a local community, in order to provide better child care services by combining available resources and establishing a suitable coordinating group such as a council, agency, or committee.

The coordinating mechanism at the federal level is the panel's 4-C Standing Committee. The regional counterpart is the Federal Regional 4-C Committee (FRC). There are committees also at the state and local levels. FRCs are in operation in the nine HEW regions. These committees selected for "pilot" programs eight states and fourteen communities specially designated to receive priority for technical assistance and funds for administration. The 4-C concept is in various stages of development in some 300 communities throughout the country.

Day Care in the District of Columbia

At the federal level alone the governmental response to public support of day care has resulted in a bewildering array of programs, some displaying considerable complexity and ambiguity. Problems of duplication and inefficiency have been recognized to some extent at the federal level, and this accounts in part for the formation of the Federal Panel on Early Childhood. But the problems associated with Title IVA and other federal grant programs are best understood by observing service delivery at the local level. For this purpose we focus on day care in the District of Columbia.

Our observations are based mainly on a field investigation of the local D.C. child care and preschool education system conducted in the summer of 1971. Interviews were held with federal and local officials, and administrators of day care associations and day care centers. Some fourteen centers of various types, including church sponsored, other private voluntary and nonprofit firms, and proprietary were visited.

Dimensions

In 1970 there were approximately 59,735 children under six in the District of Columbia. Approximately 41,302 were three-, four-, and five-year-old potential users of day care and preschool services. Of this number, approximately 15,000 are from the homes of working mothers.[4] A 1970 survey of day care in the District (the Kirschner study),[5] done at the request of the D.C. Community Health Services Administration, found that there were slightly more than 120 licensed day care centers located in the city, with a licensed capacity to serve approximately 5,000 children. More recent 1972 data indicates that the capacity of full- and half-day day care center programs has grown to approximately 9,000.[6]

At first, glance, these statistics on the supply of centers in D.C. seem contradictory to other evidence. On the one hand, the licensed capacity of centers in D.C. was a substantial fraction, about 12 percent of the total number of children eligible for day care in 1970, compared to less than 10 percent nationwide. On the other hand, the results obtained by Zamoff in the Mt. Pleasant neighborhood of Washington, D.C. (see Chapter 5) revealed that of 211 randomly chosen households with children of day care age, not one used a day care center. Thus, while the level of day care centers in D.C. is relatively high, availability at the neighborhood level seems to vary considerably. This impression is confirmed by the Kirschner study, and data from the D.C. Department of Human Resources.[7]

The day care centers in D.C. span the spectrum of organizational types including private nonprofit, private profit or propriety, voluntary and church-sponsored agencies. (There are also some public school prekindergarten programs.) Of the 120 licensed centers, the Kirschner study reported that 100 are sponsored by private and church groups, 14 by the National Capital Area Child Day Care Association (NCACDCA), 5 by United Givers Fund, one jointly funded by the National Council of Jewish Women and Georgetown University Hospital, and one supported by the District government. The Kirschner report made the following additional observations:

Centers are unevenly scattered throughout the District of Columbia; 27 are located in Northeast, 46 are located in Southeast, 44 are located in Northwest, and 3 are located in Southwest;

The 44 church-sponsored centers had an average enrollment of 40 children, as compared with 56 private centers with an average enrollment of 30.3 children;

The vast majority of day care centers are supported solely from fees collected from the families they serve. Private and church-sponsored centers are funded almost exclusively from such fees;

The cost per child in city day care centers are significantly below federal "standards." (HEW estimated that in 1968 a cost of $1,600 per child was needed to provide a "minimum" level of day care, $2,348 per child per year provided "acceptable" day care, and $2,800 per child per year "excellent" day care.) In church-sponsored centers in the District, an average of $838.70 per child is spent, and private centers spend an average of $895.85 per child. (These figures are comparable to those found in the Westinghouse study.)

How the Day Care System Works
in Washington, D.C., 1971

Funding. In 1971, the principal conduit of federal funds for day care services in the District was the Social Services Administration, an agency of the District government's Department of Human Resources, and the counterpart of the state welfare departments. Through various intra-agency programs, SSA administered four classes of funds for day care:

1. Funds for low-income (AFDC) children meeting eligibility requirements under Title IVA of the amended Social Security Act.
2. Funds for children of WIN parents (work-training program for welfare recipients) under Title IVC.

3. Child Welfare Services funds (Title IVB of the Social Security Act).
4. Model Cities Community Action Agency Funds (CAA), which flow from the Department of Housing and Urban Development to the mayor's office and finally to SSA. (Aside from Regional Commission funds, these are the only federal monies which may be used to match other federal funds, such as AFDC 25 percent matching.)

The District government utilized funds collected locally from tax revenues for its share of various matching grants, in addition to funds which were donated by voluntary agencies for the purpose of securing federal matching funds.

Private nonprofit groups seeking matching funds under Title IVA raised the 25 percent nonfederal share, navigated that share through United Givers Fund or some religious, civic, or other group, which then donated the money to the Social Services Administration. SSA then applied for 75 percent matching funds under Title IVA. The stipulation that local matching funds may not revert back to the donor agency required this type of maneuvering. For example, suppose the Washington Health and Welfare Council, a private nonprofit group and charity umbrella agency for most other charitable organizations in the District, managed to raise $10,000 through various voluntary efforts. Upon donating these funds to SSA, it would be eligible to receive $30,000 in federal matching funds to be used for day care services in one of its specific agencies; reversion of funds back to the "donor agency" is avoided by funneling the money to another branch of the Health and Welfare Council which is considered a separate entity as recipient of these funds. As another example, the Agnes Meyer Foundation may have donated $25,000 to SSA for day care, with the desire to fund a specific day care program operated by NCACDCA. The day care association would then receive $100,000 under a continuing contract with SSA.

Funds for Headstart children are directed from HEW's Office of Child Development to the local government's poverty agency in the District, the United Planning Organization. United Planning Organization contracts out services for Headstart children (to NCACDCA and others).

Until recently at least, NCACDCA seems to have provided the

most leadership in D.C. for improving the status of child care services. This association is a nonfinancially supported member of the Health and Welfare Council of Metropolitan D.C., which (as of Summer 1971) administered fourteen day care centers including one operated for the U.S. Department of Labor and another for the National Education Association. Ninety percent of children enrolled in NCACDCA centers came from families within the OEO sliding income scale, ranging from $1,800 per year for a child with one parent to $9,000 for a family of thirteen. A mother must be working, receiving training, or for some other reason be unable to care for her child, before she can place him in an NCACDCA center. In addition, children of mothers in Washington's Concentrated Employment Program who elect to move off AFDC programs and into WIN job training or placement, and children of mothers remaining on AFDC in centers funded under Title IVA's matching funds, also attend centers sponsored by NCACDCA. Theoretically, these children may not be mixed into programs other than the ones they qualify for under assistance.

Local Licensing. As of the summer 1971 one had to obtain a Certificate of Occupancy from the Department of Licensing and Inspection (L&I) and another permit from the Community Health Services Administration (CHSA) before operating a day care center in the District of Columbia. In addition, centers receiving federal subsidy must adhere to Federal Interagency Day Care Requirements.

Any change of occupancy required that a new Certificate of Occupancy be obtained. At the time of our study, the CHSA reviewed every licensed child care facility prior to permit renewal once each year after notifying the facility of the date it will be re-inspected. However, there was no legal enforcement of health regulations or any legal process for revocation of permits. L&I and CHSA followed a set procedure for coordinating their respective functions. The Social Services Administration was responsible for monitoring the quality of centers in which it placed children, but there was no systematic process for carrying this out nor was this function coordinated with the activities of CHSA or L&I.

The CHSA standards required spatial allotments of 35 square feet of inside space, and 60 square feet of outdoor space per child; the Department of Licenses and Inspections required the same indoor space, but 100 square feet of outdoor space. The Certificate of Occupancy and the health permits were issued for a stated number of children based on amount of indoor and outdoor space available, whichever allowed the smaller number of children. The CHSA inspected periodically and if violations were found to exist a letter was written by the department's supervisor to the operator of the center, demanding a reduction in the number of children served by the center. Another inspection might take place if the violation continued to exist. Beyond this, there was no enforcement mechanism.

The CHSA regulations specified only that the "health, comfort, or well-being of the inmates shall not be in danger." There was no language in the regulations concerning educational programs or qualifications of the personnel of day care centers. There are roughly 400 licensed facilities in the District which provide services to children. These include foster homes, day care centers, family day care centers, and the like. At the time of our field study, there was only one person in the CHSA responsible for licensing and inspection. It was estimated that sixty to eighty persons monthly sought information or originated requests for permits.

Local Coordination. Local coordination of day care activities in the District of Columbia is a formidable task in view of the many funding programs and agencies involved. Figure 3-1, drawn from a report by the U.S. Comptroller General to the House Committee on Education and Labor, provides a pictorial representation of this apparent complexity, caused by the fragmentation of agencies' responsibilities for day care.

Coordination of local day care is the stated objective of the D.C. 4-C agency. This agency is designed to be broadly representative of the various factions in the city that are concerned with day care. The agency has two governing bodies, an Assembly of Agencies and a Board of Directors elected by the Assembly. The board consists of fifteen parents whose children are served by local day care programs, seventeen representatives of organizations which supply day care services, seven members who are elected representatives of organizations which control public and/or private funds for child care services, and six members appointed by various city agencies.

The 4-C goal of local coordination is broadly proclaimed to

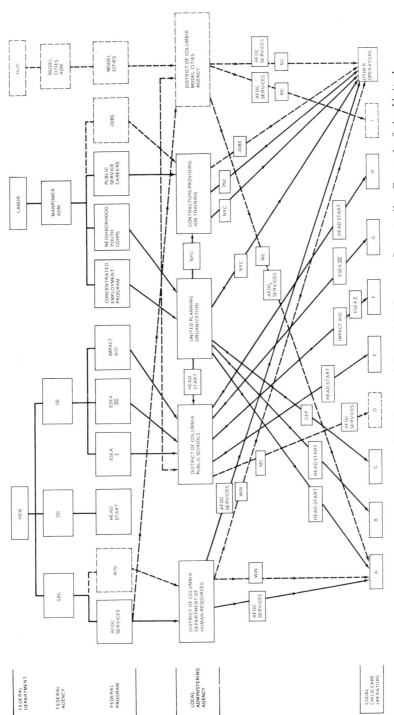

Figure 3-1. Child-Care Activities in the District of Columbia. Source: Comptroller General of the United States, "Study of Child-Care Activities in the District of Columbia," Report to the Committee on Education and Labor, U.S. House of Representatives; reprinted from *Voice for Children*, vol. 5, no. 3, (March 1972).

include planning, implementation of standards, and resource allocation on a communitywide basis, as well as consolidation of financial transactions for securing and distributing federal funds. But the agency has had a rocky history. Although 4-C has put much effort into coalescing the many day care interests in the city, there was great initial reluctance on the part of private and church-sponsored groups to participate. Some viewed 4-C as an attempt to impose impractical or unprofitable standards. District officials expressed fear that private operators would belong to 4-C strictly as a means of obtaining federal funds. In 1971 the 4-C agency applied to HEW for "full recognition" as the official community agency for all day care programs in the District of Columbia. In response, the D.C. City Council legislated into existence the Division of Child Development (DCD) under the D.C. Department of Human Resources, to assume responsibility for coordinating day care in the District.

D.C. Revisited

It must be noted that the foregoing observations on local licensing and funding in Washington, D.C., are now out of date. Nevertheless, they may serve to indicate the kinds of situations occurring in other localities. So, too, the changes that have been made in D.C. since the summer of 1971 may be of interest elsewhere. Since 1971 the CHSA responsibilities for day care have been assumed by a Division of Licensing and Standards (DLS) in the D.C. Department of Human Resources and renewed attention has been given to the licensing and inspection functions. DLS now coordinates the activities of the several local agencies which share responsibility for licensing day care facilities. The names of some of these agencies have also changed:

1. The Bureau of Building Housing and Zoning, (BHZ) issues a Certificate of Occupany for the proposed site of a day care facility after inspections for plumbing, building and electrical code violations;
2. The Bureau of Community and Institutional Hygiene sets standards related to food handling and other health problems;
3. The Fire Marshall's Office has responsibility to insure that facilities are in compliance with fire safety regulations;

4. The Social Rehabilitation Administration's (formerly SSA) interest is that federal standards for child care financed by federal funds are complied with.

DLS itself inspects and enforces its own standards for day care operation, as well as those set by the Social Rehabilitation Administration, the Bureau of Community and Institutional Hygiene, and the Fire Marshall. The usual procedure for obtaining a permit to operate a child care facility is as follows: a prospective day care operator locates a facility for his program. He then calls DLS which arranges for a pre-inspection appointment. (DLS also urges the caller to attend its biweekly orientation session for prospective day care operators, which deals with issues of program content in addition to licensing requirements and standards.) The prospective operator then applies to the BHZ for a Certificate of Occupancy. If the site meets BHZ standards the certificate is issued and the center may begin to hire staff, enroll children, obtain equipment, and prepare to operate. If the standards of the DLS and the three other agencies are then met, the DLS issues a permit to operate and the center may go into business.

The Certificate of Occupancy expires only upon a change in location or ownership, but the Permit to Operate must be renewed annually. Unscheduled re-inspection visits are made by DLS approximately two months prior to the expiration date. The three DLS inspectors perform thirty to forty day care center pre-inspections per month, and a minimum of four unscheduled "drop in" visits per year, with inspections averaging from an hour to an hour and a half.

In conjunction with the foregoing changes in licensing and inspection procedures, the District has taken greater responsibility for funding and coordinating day care. Rather than leaving the initiative completely to local providers, the new Division of Child Development now actively seeks out grant applicants, helps secure matching funds, and attempts to coordinate and exploit the use of an array of (grant) revenue sources to address the needs for day care services throughout the city. There is some feeling in DCD that the District of Columbia may have a special advantage in pursuing such activities because of its unique status as a city and a state, which provides special opportunities both to control funds locally, and to become intimately familiar with local groups. Thus funding power can be skillfully used as leverage to encourage changes in local supply. The potency of this funding leverage may be sorely tested now that Title IVA has been severely limited.

Assessment of the Present Delivery System for Publicly Supported Day Care

Several factors conspire to limit the effectiveness of publicly supported day care programs, and to inhibit the local day care sector from responding to the needs of the community. These factors may be conveniently classified into three levels: the system level, the grant program level, and the supplier level.

System Level Problems

One immediate impression of the present delivery system is the disjointed, fragmentary, and rigid nature of federal grant programs. Child care centers funded under separate federal programs find themselves competing with each other for children in certain eligibility categories and geographic locations, while children in other categories or locations go unserved. The fragmentation of agency responsibility for different child care programs leads to other problems for consumers of day care services. In particular, it is often extremely difficult for parents to learn what options are available for child care. Knowledge about day care programs is communicated ineffectively by advertisements or word-of-mouth. NCACDCA has its guides and brochures for its specific group of programs, and Catholic Charities has its own packaged advertisements. But no public or private agency assumes responsibility for dissemination of comprehensive information on local day care opportunities.

Another implication of system fragmentation is the difficulty many day care suppliers face in obtaining public subsidy funds. Day care "entrepreneurs" are faced with multiple burdens of finding sources of support, administering programs, and managing facilities. If these entrepreneurs are to vigorously pursue the goal of supplying day care to low- and moderate-income children they must become facile in manipulating the system of federal grants in order to secure the necessary subsidies for program development and expansion. But the nature of the federal grant programs is hostile to all but the most sophisticated suppliers. The fragmentation of federal programs provides a confusing array of funding sources, each with different specifications, and matching requirements that vary from 25 percent to 0 percent as we have seen. Complying with Federal Interagency Day Care Requirements and local licensing standards can be a complex process. Having to fathom the system of funding, standards, audits, and reviews can be discouraging and defeating to the applicant, and seems to have created disincentives to expansion, or initiation of new programs. As the ABT study concluded:

Our chief finding about start-up was to illuminate the enormous effort required to start a center. At least one aggregate person-year of work is needed to get a center going. Growth costs are similar: it takes great energy to recruit sufficient resources for survival, much less stable growth.[8]

As the task of obtaining support for child care services is extremely difficult for all but the most sophisticated suppliers, the large established providers tend to take on greater and greater shares of service provision. This fact alone would seem to have important implications for the vitality of the local day care sector. One director who tried faithfully to obtain federal funds, but finally secured borrowed funds to open his center, commented that "NCACDCA seems to have sucked up all of the available funds."

Seemingly, NCACDCA and other established groups such as United Givers Fund and Catholic charities dominate the funding sources because of their familiarity with the grant process. The more established providers seem to have well-working liaisons with appropriate officials. Licensing requirements, matching funds, and supportive services are easier for them to acquire than for smaller nonprofit and proprietary groups without these liaisons. Supportive services which may be obtained free through various programs and donors are unknown to many of the private nonprofit centers not operating under NCACDCA's auspices. This situation would seem to have important implications in terms of locking in current suppliers and excluding new and potentially innovative approaches.

Given the difficulties of entry by new independent providers, supply response is limited by the inertia of the current large providers, who dominate the funding sources. On the other hand, the organized approach of associations such as NCACDCA *is* one way of coping with the complexity of the existing system of funding and regulations. Without such organizations the supply problem might well be worse. Nevertheless the situation facing smaller suppliers is a serious one, perhaps best summed up this way:

Here, as in most areas of Social Policy, we are involved in a giant grantsmanship game. The game board is set up to force local people to puzzle out their moves through the maze to funds which may have been used up by the time the application arrives.[9]

Hence, the extent and quality of actual services may depend more on the competence of local agencies and groups to thread the maze, than on the local community's desire for child care services.

Basically, problems at the system level are ones of coordination— among grant programs, funding and licensing agencies, and current and potential day care suppliers and users. Attempts to provide coordination, for purposes of improved efficiency, resource allocation, and quality control, have so far been faltering and piecemeal. Most prominently, the 4-C program has met with mixed reactions, with hostility in some localities, and apparent indifference and lack of support at the federal level. In particular, HEW has not sought to exploit the 4-C mechanism to coordinate its own programs, or to consolidate funding, information dissemination, or standards enforcement procedures at the local level.[10] In Washington, D.C., attempts by the local 4-C to enlarge its own role in coordinating local day care inspired a countermove by the City Council to establish an agency responsible for day care coordination within the local government structure.

Whether 4-C is the appropriate mechanism for attempting to coordinate the system of publicly supported day care is open to question. For example, the nature of the coordinating functions such as consolidation of the funding and licensing processes, suggest that an executive type agency within local government like DCD would perhaps be a less controversial and perhaps more vigorous vehicle for undertaking these tasks. Yet 4-C, as an agency broadly representative of the various day care interests in the city, would appear to fill an important advisory and policymaking capacity, as well as providing some coordination among different child-related interests and programs. As we shall discuss, parent and citizen overview and participation seem essential to successful regulation of the day care sector, and councils with a representative structure like 4-C should have a key part in making these mechanisms operative. Furthermore, it is clear that a serious mistake would be made if 4-C were simply ignored or disbanded. For local 4-C efforts represent the hard work of citizens dedicated to improving child care in their communities. It would seem worthwhile to transform 4-C into an effective component of the system, in order to exploit the energies of the existing day care constituencies.

Individual Grant Programs

If the constellation of public programs and regulatory requirements for day care as a whole is problematic, so is the nature of some of the individual grant programs. For example, the inflexibility of particular programs, i.e., the fact that program monies are specifically tied to tightly defined adult-oriented purposes, results in inefficient use of available facilities and discontinuity of child care when adult circumstances change. Nonworking mothers, for example, cannot switch from nonworking to working status without shifting their children from one program to another. Children of WIN mothers receiving services may not be mixed with children of CEP or Model Cities groups, even if such programs are nearer to home and more convenient for mother and child. Each child must attend the center supported by funds of his respective program. And programs such as CEP do not provide for the continued financing of day care after a parent completes a manpower training program. Thus, families who have qualified for subsidized day care during a period of a training program may lose their eligibility once the training program is over. To continue to use the day care would require payment of fees which they may not be able to afford.

Other aspects of individual grant programs have also been troublesome, especially with respect to the responsiveness of day care supply. For example, while recent administrative interpretation would seem to have cleared up much of the problem, the "statewideness" requirement of the Title IVA program has caused confusion in the past among those wishing to start pilot or experimental programs for AFDC recipients, because a state usually cannot offer such services to every eligible person in every geographic area. A second problem with Title IVA has been the uncertainty of whether Title IVA money would remain open-ended. Many states have been reluctant to become involved with Title IVA because of the fear that they will be left with full responsibility for the program at some future time. Some states' entire welfare program would be jeopardized if the costs of federal matching shares had to be assumed. These fears have been justified by the 1972 federal revenue-sharing legislation which has clamped a tight lid on Title IVA appropriations.

Finally, we find the rules governing matching funds and purchase of services under Title IVA sometimes conflict with state laws. Most states have long-standing procedures regarding conversion of private to public monies and contracting for services. As a result, some states have failed in the past to fully exploit Title IVA as a source of funds for day care and other social services.

Despite the proliferation of guidelines and regulations federal day care grant programs are also notable for their ambiguity on what funds may be used for. The phrase to note in most of the grant program descriptions is "funds *may* be used."[11] The uncertainty of whether a proposed day care program does or does not qualify for grant funds puts the negotiating skill and guile of fund-seekers at a premium.

Finally, even when grant funds are secured, problems associated with program operation remain. Day care center directors, for example, are still caught in the constraints of the annual governmental budget cycle, even if provisions exist for amending contracts in mid-year to account for special circumstances. Asked what they would do if the center needed a major piece of equipment or additional supplies, directors at federally supported centers responded that they would have to wait until next year's budget application before they would even make such requests.

Day Care Suppliers

Clearly, another important factor affecting the supply of day care is the particular nature of the individuals upon whom heavy reliance is placed for initiating and delivering day care programs. The directors of many supplying agencies, both nonprofit and proprietary, are service rather than profit oriented. They are in business to see that children receive wholesome care, not especially for the financial returns. Our impression is that such individuals are generally absorbed with trying to provide programs of good quality for their own clientele, but are less interested in growth, or in responding to demands for additional capacity. Their standards remain high, their waiting lists grow, but their inclination to service these unmet demands is weak. While this is reassuring insofar as the treatment of enrolled children is concerned, it points to the need for some mechanism to stimulate supply to be responsive to outstanding demands for day care services.

On the other hand, there is no assurance that all day care suppliers are so dedicated or scrupulous in their approach to treatment of children. To the contrary, many centers and day care homes have been found to be in abominable conditions.[1 2] Yet, the existing system of monitoring and inspection, licensing and regulation is not capable of effectively controlling quality of day care services either. A reformed delivery system for day care will have to address this aspect of service performance as well.

Conclusion

In summary, we observe an ill-coordinated and rather cumbersome and entangling delivery system for publicly supported day care, which provides weak assurances of quality care, and mutes the incentives for supply to adjust to demand. Difficulties of federal program fragmentation, ambiguities in the administration of individual grant programs, budgeting and financial constraints, closed funding channels, and disparate licensing requirements point to the need for streamlining and consolidating governmental finance and regulatory machinery for day care. But even more than this is needed. The eleemosynary nature of many day care suppliers suggests that some supplementary organizational mechanism is necessary to stimulate the rate at which the backlog of day care needs is addressed. At the same time, the sensitive character of child care requires an organizational structure that will ensure an adequate quality of services provided by such trustworthy institutions. In our next chapter, we develop the conceptual foundation and a basic organizational framework that we believe would take these considerations into proper account.

4

Two Major Issues of Public Policy: Public Subsidy and Organization of Supply

Richard Nelson and
Michael Krashinsky

Introduction

As we have already noted, what is particularly striking about the present system of public support for day care is its multiplicity of purposes—relating to poverty and welfare, training and employment, and education and child development—and the fragmentation of federal programs that this has produced. The national debate over proposed new day care programs exhibits the same diversity of objectives, as illustrated by recently considered child development legislation on the one hand and welfare reform legislation on the other hand. These proposals call for significant increases in federal funds, and some potentially significant changes in the organization of day care. But the diversity in sources of support for something called day care is indicative more of agreement about words than about real things. There is a very real tension, for example, between the "free mothers to work" arguments for day care and other arguments that stress a program for children, whether or not their parents work, and perhaps even regardless of the income of the parents. Such tensions must be resolved in order to develop a sensible and coherent public policy for subsidizing day care.

Establishing the proper objectives for public support of day care is important not only for developing a coherent subsidy policy, but for untying some of the organizational tangles that currently hinder the provision of publicly supported day care. We saw earlier that the present regime of public subsidy and local regulation, fragmented in part because of the variety of day care interests, discourages new suppliers, fails to coordinate needs or demands for day care with

---

This chapter is based on Richard R. Nelson and Michael Krashinsky, "Some Questions of Optimal Organization: The Case of Day Care for Children," Urban Institute Working Paper 1205-2, December 1971.

existing sources of supply, and provides uncertain assurances that reasonable levels of quality will be maintained. But we also discovered that the tangled machinery of public day care program administration is not solely responsible for these supply problems. The peculiarities of day care suppliers as economic agents, and the inherent nature of day care as a service, seem to require special attention with regard to the appropriate form of public regulation and control. The organization of day care looms as an extremely important public policy issue, separable from, but related to, subsidy policy.

Public Subsidy Policy

What are the valid arguments for public subsidy of day care, and what should be the form of the subsidy? One view of day care argues for day care subsidy to enable poor mothers to work and earn a living. Unfortunately, this rationale would appear to confuse a number of issues. Clearly, raising the incomes of the poor is a most important objective. Equally clearly, if parents work and cannot take adequate care of their children, it is important that government try to assure that the children have decent care. But the latter objective would seem to hold regardless of whether or not the parents are working. And the former would seem best met by assuring a decent guaranteed income and opportunity to earn more. If higher family income is the sole objective, the family should have the incentive to use day care if the income that would be earned by work force participation exceeds the cost of extra family child care, otherwise not. For families with a small number of young children and a high earning potential, day care makes economic sense from this point of view. For large families where the mother has limited earning potential, day care looks like bad economics and a simple money check looks better.[1]

It seems far more sensible to view public support of day care as a service for children of poor families or for children in general. Instead of viewing young children as an obstacle to a mother's working and hence earning a decent income (as seems implicit in the welfare reform discussion of day care) the more appropriate perspective is to consider the often grossly unsatisfactory conditions for children of poor families when the mother works. The requirement for public policy is simply the obligation of a society to the well-being of its young children. It is unlikely that federally supported day care programs will, over the next decade, provide adequate care for all children of poor families in which parents are required to or choose to work. It seems impossible that such an objective can be achieved if increasing the number of working mothers is an end in itself. It would therefore seem that a key part of a program aimed at improving child care should be a guaranteed annual income to poor families with no artificial encouragement for the mothers to work outside the household. If the mother chooses to work, she should be free to do so and the marginal tax rate should be low. (And day care costs certainly should be deductible from income for tax purposes, as a legitimate expense of holding an outside job.) But one of the purposes of the guaranteed annual income, regardless of employment, is to free the mother of any need to work and of the requirement to leave her children in some other kind of care. Day care facilities should be available for her children, but any *subsidization* of day care services should reflect appraisal of the care the children would get at the center relative to what they would get at home. Or, given that many mothers will choose to work, *subsidy* should provide encouragement to place the children at a center that provides quality care rather than in an arrangement that uses fewer resources and is worse for the child.

This perspective has the advantage of not treating asymmetrically, or worse, as a completely separate issue, the question of public subsidy of day care for children of families above the poverty line. The issue here, as for the children of poor families, is: would the children be better off if more facilities are made available and, if so, would public subsidy induce parents to make as much use of good day care as they should. One can argue that the home care of a child of a well-off family is likely to be better than that of a poverty family and hence the benefits to the child of extra-family care in the former case, are likely to be fewer, or even negative. If the mother chooses to work she will likely choose to provide him with good care, in a day care center or otherwise, so that no subsidy is needed. The thrust of this argument is that the subsidy for day care should decrease as family income increases and perhaps drop to zero at some point. But one does not need to somehow view day care for the poor and nonpoor as completely separate questions. While the answer regarding the level of public subsidy is different, the public policy question is the same for both groups of children.

From this perspective it certainly makes sense for the federal government to subsidize day care in those circumstances where parents choose to work, but where parental resources would buy inadequate care. There is a dilemma here, of course, since subsidizing care will stimulate the demand for child care and the motivation of mothers to work. There is some evidence that such a stimulative effect may not be large, however.[2] Nonetheless, subsidy and other government policy ought to aim at ensuring that in such cases, the day care provided is equal or superior to the care the children would have received at home, at least in those dimensions where resources count.

There also is justification for government subsidy of day care, even where parents do not work, *if* such subsidization is necessary for children to receive the care that society deems they should. Such subsidy clearly is justified in cases where children otherwise would be neglected or their development hindered. But it is unclear just how many children would benefit, and to what degree, by having them attend day care programs rather than stay with their parents. And it is not certain how (or whether) benefits to children increase significantly with expenditures on preschool services. This is not the place to attempt a comprehensive review of the state of research on the effects of preschool programs on the development of children. In brief, however, our understanding is that there is no clear-cut evidence that highly resource-intensive preschool services have a major impact on the development of children. To consider just one dimension of human development, cognitive ability, the recent report on education and inequality by Jencks et al. summarizes evidence from the Equality of Educational Opportunity Survey and other sources, as follows:

Once socio-economic differences were taken into account, there were no significant differences in sixth grade achievement between those who said they had attended nursery school and those who said they had not. Given the probable inaccuracies in the data, this finding is hardly conclusive, but it is consistent with most other surveys and experimental research on pre-schooling.

Follow-ups of pre-school alumni have a long history. They fall into a predictable pattern. The majority show that children who attend pre-school do quite a lot better on standardized tests at the end of their pre-school year than children who did not attend pre-school. But children who do not attend pre-school usually catch up with children who do attend by the end of the first grade. Only one or two small studies claim appreciable differences beyond first grade.

The largest single follow-up of pre-school alumni was the 1968 Westinghouse-Ohio survey of Headstart graduates. This study concluded that neither year-round nor summer Headstart programs had a significant long-term effect on children's cognitive growth. When we reanalyzed this data, we found a few year-round centers in which the Headstart children's advantage over non-Headstart children persisted through first grade. Beyond first grade, however, the picture was gloomy. Overall, the evidence strongly suggested that Headstart's effects on children's cognitive growth had been quite transitory.[3]

Of course, focusing on cognitive ability is much too narrow a position, for human development has many other dimensions. Unfortunately, reliable research tools have not yet been developed to measure other equally important aspects such as the child's creative or artistic abilities or his feelings about himself and his relationships with others. Thus, if we are uncertain about benefits in terms of cognitive learning, we are even less sure of benefits along other dimensions of development. But the uncertainties associated with education benefits from preschool programs do not contradict the rationale we have suggested for subsidizing day care—that of ensuring children a reasonably good level of care, and avoiding deteriorations in care when parents decide to work and put their children into day care. However, the uncertain state of knowledge about child benefits does bring into question whether very expensive programs are justified. In particular, when considered in conjunction with probable limitations on the magnitude of public appropriations for day care, our uncertainty about child benefits calls attention to what is perhaps the most controversial question regarding day care subsidy: Should federal subsidy involve large expenditure per child, in which case it is highly unlikely that the subsidy will be able to cover all applicant children? Or should federal subsidy per child be smaller, but coverage greater? Two basic questions are involved in determining a desirable level of subsidy: the total expenditure level per child in day care which government should be willing to support (or guarantee), and the proportion of that cost which should be covered by subsidy (rather than by user fees).

If day care of reasonably good quality were totally financed by a (limited) appropriation of government funds, program coverage would inevitably be restricted. If parents pay part of the cost through user fees, however, government funds can be spread out to cover more children in subsidized day care. These considerations argue for a fee (and subsidy) schedule for day care high enough to provide substantial revenues, but graduated by family income to avoid substantial resistance to usage when such usage is in the interests of the child. Survey results discussed in Chapter 5 indicate that 20 percent to 30 percent of household per capita income may be a reasonable range for fees which parents are willing to pay for extra-family day care.

However, the more basic question is: what level of day care quality (expenditure per child) should government support. The centers in the Westinghouse sample spent an average of $650 per child per year. Certainly good care costs more than this. But a figure like $2300 for desirable day care proposed by the Office of Child Development (in 1968 prices), especially if it were financed mostly by government, would virtually guarantee that a national subsidy program will have very limited coverage, as the required massive federal appropriations are not likely to be forthcoming.[4]

The question of day care expenditure level hinges on the range and quality of services provided through subsidized day care arrangements. It is useful to separate day care, conceptually, into two components, "basic day care" and "supplements" to basic care. We have argued that at a minimum, subsidized extra-family day care should provide a level of care at least as good as the routine care which attending children would have received at home. This would be our "basic" level of care. Unfortunately, the concept of basic care, phrased in this manner, is elusive. For in certain dimensions no level of expenditure or program design can substitute for parental care. In addition, unless the expenditure level for day care is very high, there will be no guarantee that some children, e.g., those from unusually good homes, will not experience a deterioration in care if they are placed in extra-family day care, even in dimensions where resources do count. Thus, a level of care which generally represents an improvement for most children may constitute a deterioration for other children. Thus, to be pragmatic, it is necessary to talk in terms of a basic "guarantee level" on which the public (or experts?) can agree provides an adequate level of care, generally regarded to be a satisfactory substitute for what children would otherwise receive.

The cost of this basic level of care would have to take into account a desired staff/child ratio, level of staff competence, minimum facility standards, and certain basic auxiliary services such as food and minimum health care (first aid).

We have no precise idea about what this expenditure level should be. There is some consensus among "experts" that a staff/child ratio on the order of 5 to 1 is "desirable," where staff is a mixture of professional and nonprofessional people. In addition to program staff requirements, which are the overwhelming elements in terms of cost, minimum levels of other budget items such as administration and building occupancy costs would seem to be necessary for quality care. Perhaps the best material available is the small scale study by Abt Associates for the Office of Economic Opportunity.[5] Based on a sampling of twenty day care centers generally regarded as having reputations for good quality care, this study estimated that good quality basic care, pricing volunteer resources at market prices, cost in the neighborhood of $2200 per child (in 1970). For the centers that were studied, an average of almost 25 percent of "revenues" were in the form of unpaid resources. This factor, plus the Abt study's selection process, which seems clearly biased upwards in the quality dimension, would argue for deflating the given cost figure for quality care. It seems reasonable that good care could be provided for under $2000.

A public day care policy should, at a minimum, strive to support such a basic level of expenditure. But beyond this level, one which substitutes for good home care by parents, what should subsidized day care attempt to provide? There are a number of possible supplements to basic day care which may provide additional benefits to children. These would include medical and dental care, special educational materials and equipment, field trips, professional entertainment, musical instruments and instruction, foreign language instruction, and so on. Such supplements may require the services of doctors, nurses, and other outside professionals, and a day care staff competence and staff/child ratio above what is required for basic care. In general, greater expenditure per child would be necessary.

However, it is important to realize that day care need not be the exclusive vehicle for delivering many of these supplemental services to children. This is quite apparent for something like medical services, but even for educational supplements there are other vehicles such as television or training of parents to provide educational experiences in the home. Indeed, it would be blatantly inequitable to provide such supplemental services only to children in day care, and fail to provide them to children who do not attend day care. In addition, the provision (and subsidy) of some of these supplements through day care exclusively may induce some parents to place their children in day care for the wrong reason. For in some circumstances, a child might be better off at home if subsidized supplemental services were available elsewhere than through day care.

But most important to this discussion, loading supplements heavily onto basic day care will, in the context of limited public appropriations for day care subsidy, restrict the availability of subsidized day care to relatively few children. It is this argument that leads us to the conclusion that the level of expenditure per child which public subsidy of day care should support, should be "basic day care plus," i.e., a level which society judges to be a reasonable substitute for the care children would otherwise receive, plus a minimal supplement of extra services (some educational materials, field trips, perhaps annual medical checkups, etc.) which do not inflate costs much beyond this basic level.

To avoid any misinterpretation, it must be stressed that this position does *not* oppose the provision of subsidized medical and dental care and other specialized services to children. In fact, special legislation to provide such benefits to children, in *and* out of the day care context, would be welcome. Indeed, a scheme of subsidy to "basic day care plus" could conceivably be coupled with separate programs of subsidy for more intensive supplemental services for all children. In particular, one can conceive of a "voucher" arrangement under which parents are given separate tickets for day care and for supplemental services. If a parent chose to place his child in day care, he or she could spend the supplemental vouchers in the day care context. Otherwise, the certificates could be used elsewhere. Our concern in separating the subsidy for supplements from the subsidy for day care is the limited availability of good day care that would result from high expenditures per child for day care per se.

A voucher-like arrangement (which may or may not involve physical paper certificates), in which the subsidy is tied to the child rather than the supplier of services, is attractive in the day care context for a number of other reasons relating to fundamental issues of day care organization. It is to this subject that we turn next.

Organization of the Supply of Day Care

A sensible general public policy towards subsidy (and related standards and eligibility guidelines) for day care is only a paper construction in the absence of effective organizational arrangements to interpret and carry it out. In an effort to analyze alternative organizational modes, our discussion here centers on how two essential processes work under different organizational regimes. One is the *evaluation* process. This is the mechanism by which the performance of. the day care sector as a whole and that of its subunits are assessed in terms of benefits and costs, and how the results of this assessment are somehow communicated to the agencies responsible for supply. In different organizational regimes, different groups and mechanisms are involved in the evaluation. Benefits and costs are assessed from different perspectives and felt by the suppliers in different ways. The other process is that of *supply adjustment* to the evaluation. Again this works differently under different organizational arrangements. In the remainder of this section, various stylized arrangements are considered and some widely held prejudices explored. This leads to a proposal for organizing day care, discussed in the next section.

The Problems with Private Enterprise
and the Market

There appears to be near-consensus among persons who write about day care that private for-profit enterprise and the "market" is an unsatisfactory way of organizing this activity. Interestingly enough, the belief seems to be held by many businessmen as well as by day care officials.[6] Essentially unregulated private enterprise today provides a significant fraction of day care. It is apparent that most day care specialists consider this an unfortunate fact of life signifying the undersupply of more adequate forms of day care. Even regulated private enterprise is suspect. Relatedly there is a deep suspicion of for-profit nursing homes and hospitals. Clearly profit is being mentally associated with exploitation rather than with responsible service. This may appear somewhat strange in a country where private enterprise solutions tend to be exalted. What lies behind the apparent rejection?

Unregulated private enterprise—the market—performs the evaluative function by individual consumers deciding what and what not to buy. The supply adjustment is performed by firms seeking profit. One of the more obvious problems with this regime, in pure form, is that it does not take into account the public interest in quality child care. It is apparent that many Americans believe that children of poor families ought to have better care than their parents will choose, or can afford, to purchase. It would be simple enough, however, to supplement private enterprise with subsidy if this were the only complication. Individual consumers (parents) would still evaluate day care arrangements and make their evaluations effective by giving or withholding patronage. Public subsidy would influence the response of suppliers to consumer choice by making it more profitable for firms to have more customers of a particular kind than would be the case without subsidy.

However, there is a more basic objection to private enterprise. Although we have not seen this spelled out explicitly, there is a widespread feeling that private enterprise is not to be trusted, that the control exercised by consumer choice is not likely to be sharp-eyed or well informed about what is best for the children, and that the social responsibility in this matter requires better control than consumer choice and private free enterprise will provide.[7]

Day care is provided largely when the parents are not present. And while their reactions may be solicited, children are not themselves qualified to evaluate the service. There are, therefore, no easily observable objective facts on which to base evaluation. It is clear then that *trust* must play an enormous role in day care provision. How does a parent really know what kind of day care a child is getting at a day care center? The provision of day care within the family neatly bypasses this problem. The extension of the family to involve relatives in child care operations involves similar machinery. The mechanism is similar when close friends are asked to babysit or when a group of friends or neighbors establishes a babysitting pool. Trust and mutual interest enable the system to work. What happens when a day care center is set up and run by people with whom the family has no close bonds? The possibility of occasional sampling plus reports from the child give some assurance that truly horrendous care will not be the rule. But beyond this how is the parent to judge? If a parent cannot judge, how is the competitive market supposed to work?

In some of the discussions of day care a somewhat different stress is placed on the problem. It is argued that the parents do not know what kind of care and environment is best for their children.[8] The stress here is on the lack of expertise rather than problems of display. But the conclusion regarding the inadequacy of "market" evaluation is the same.

The problem is, of course, compounded if public subsidy is to be provided. The public, like the individual parent, wants value for its money. But if a parent cannot judge quality there is no assurance that public funds are accomplishing anything. They may go straight from the public treasury to the pocket of the day care center without influencing the service provided. It is clear that worries of this sort are reflected in past policies that have been biased against providing subsidized day care funds to proprietary centers.

In theory, the profit-oriented economic institution is not supposed to be concerned directly with the quality of its output but only with its profit. Normally, appropriate quality is seen to be automatically guaranteed by the operation of the market—consumers do not buy shoddy items, so quality becomes a necessary condition for profit. But when display is a problem and when moreover there exist no easily quantifiable measurements of output, the link may be broken. Suppose taking good care of children yields lower profit than providing inferior care by cutting costs in ways that are not easily seen by parents? If consumer choice is defective as an evaluation device, yet is the principal determinant of profitability, then an adjustment process keyed to profitability poses a serious problem.

This is at the basis of the widespread belief and enactment into state law that day care facilities, particularly proprietary ones, should be regulated and licensed by some responsible public body. Under such a regime the evaluative function is shared by consumer choice and governmental specification of certain constraints. However, regulation at best has its problems. It is easier to enforce the letter of the law than to assure that the purpose of the law is met; there are far too many ways to scrimp on day care to be sanguine about ruling out all of these legally. The problem is compounded by the costs of regulation per se. While gross deficiencies can be avoided with a reasonable commitment of regulatory agency staff, it is not reasonable to expect that exhaustive close coverage can be achieved through conventional regulatory machinery. These considerations lie behind the apparent beliefs of many day care specialists that even regulated private enterprise is a dangerous mode of day care organization.

It may be objected that this view of private enterprise is too harsh and that private parties providing day care do so largely because they enjoy caring for children and feel this is an important job. A living is a constraint, not the principal objective. There is reason to believe that this may be so with respect to many proprietary day care centers. But if this is the motivation then the mode of sectoral organization cannot be characterized by the traditional competitive model. Further, if profits are not the driving force, then we lose many of the arguments for profit-oriented provision as the optimal arrangement. If the "better" firm does not make larger profits and expand and drive out the "poorer" firm many of the benefits of competition are lost.

In short, it seems that the basic evaluation and adjustment mechanism of consumer choice plus profit-oriented private enterprise is not well suited to the needs of controlling day care, and cannot easily be patched up by subsidy to take account of the public interest in the service, and by regulation to take care of the overview problem. The basic problem is that since individual customers are not sharp-eyed judges of quality of service, and because quality is very important, a mechanism of strongly profit-guided supply response is dangerous. This suggests that day care should be provided by organizations that are motivated by considerations that go beyond profit.

A Lack of Enthusiasm for Public Provision

It is interesting that outside the public school establishment advocacy for the provision of day care through a public agency is not widespread.[9] And in public education, of course, there has been some movement away from public provision. State welfare departments and education departments do run day care centers, but according to the Westinghouse survey these are a small proportion of the total. State welfare departments often take care of their day care needs by contracting with nonprofit agencies. While some proposed legislation would channel funds through state government agencies, it does not seem the intention to have state agencies set up and run day care centers. If private enterprise is not to be trusted, the idea of providing day care through government departments is at best a depressing alternative.

Public enterprise does have the dual advantages of having the system run by public officials who, partially at least, can be selected and influenced to operate the system in the public interest and not for a quick dollar, and of having subsidy built in. The key problem is how the public interest is to be defined and how evaluation is to be brought to bear on that process in a way that influences the provision of day care.

In a system of public provision individual choice among alternatives is muted if not actually scotched. Judgments of individual consumers are executed through votes on key issues, choice of representatives to whom decision is delegated, and direct and indirect pressure on the bureaucracy that runs the system of individual centers. Thus, the consumer evaluation mechanism is largely through "voice" rather than "exit," i.e., complaints and pressures brought against one's present supplier rather than abandonment of this supplier in favor of another, to use Albert Hirschman's concepts.[10] In a system of public provision, professional judgment can be brought into the evaluative process at a higher level than in a completely decentralized system through studies and evaluations. If the arguments about the lack of consumer expertise are accepted, this is an advantage of the evaluative system under public provision. However, lack of scientific understanding about what really is good day care, or value consensus on what "good" means, or how to measure these things, implies that the formal evaluation of experts cannot be relied on as the dominant mechanism of evaluation. And exactly how such collective machinery is to mesh with direct citizen pressure and voting is not clear.

Public provision of a roughly uniform model of day care with no consumer choice among alternative centers seems quite unacceptable. Almost all of the evaluation burden then, is placed on collective and professional judgment machinery, and collective decision machinery grinds slow and jerkily. Further, while a private enterprise regime perhaps places too much weight on the judgments and felt needs of individual families, the regime of public provision of this sort tends to place too little weight on individual judgment, if experience with the public school system is any guide.

As has been proposed for public schools, providing families with a range of choice among public institutions can provide more consumer weight to the evaluation process. However, as Downs has pointed out (in the case of school reform) for increased consumer choice to be effective, modifications need to be made in the traditional public sector adjustment machinery.[11] The traditional public sector adjustment machinery is centralized to a considerable degree. The results of evaluation effect action through a set of commands from high public officials to members of the public bureaucracy. In order for consumer "exit" to have influence, individual center directors must have some motivation to attract more children. They must have the freedom to vary programs to try to make their centers more attractive. If they are successful they must be able to get resources to enable them to expand and meet higher demands; if they lose customers their resources must be cut back. The requirements are for a reward structure, a mode of decentralized authority, and a budget machinery quite foreign to public sector provision as we now know it. No one has yet come up with an attractive proposal as to how to make such a system work.

Day Care Cooperatives and Not-for-Profits

In view of the apparent shortcomings in obtaining day care through private enterprise or a public agency, the idea of providing it through cooperation is very attractive. If individual families become less able or willing to provide care for their own children directly, one might think that communities could work out arrangements cooperatively, without formal public organization. At first glance it seems plausible that groups of parents ought to be able to get together and provide cooperative day care for their children, by sharing the work and assuring good care through mutual trust and collective overview.

However, there are severe difficulties with a pure cooperative model which surely rule it out as a general solution. Cooperatives are hard to put together, and when they are put together they tend to be cumbersome for decisionmaking, prone to slacking on the part of cooperative members, and unstable. Consider the difficulties even relatively close friends have in squaring accounts in babysitting exchange arrangements when the needs of one couple are significantly larger than the needs of the other over an extended period of time. Various forms of side payment are possible—taking the other couple out to dinner, or various gifts. But the longer these continue the more implausible it is that what is going on is a babysitting cooperative rather than one couple employing another to babysit for them.

With a large number of families in a child care cooperative, symmetry of needs is virtually impossible. The cooperative tends to break up into those who care for the children and those who use day care and then compensate the day care workers by other means, almost certainly money payment. This is even more necessary if the cooperative is to be viewed by those in need of day care as a place where they can always leave their children. Small babysitting cooperatives of the sort generated by friendly couples are notoriously unreliable in that no couple can be assured that the other couple will be available when needed. A group of day care workers is going to have to be paid for providing day care. While there may be volunteers, and mothers who "pay" for the care given their children by giving some of their own time to the center, and even a number of pure coops, the pure cooperative idea is chimerical as the central organizing principle for a general system of extra-family day care. The "impure" cooperative day care systems that do succeed are able to do so because they use paid help to achieve a balance between demands placed on parent's services, and the cost and quality of care desired.

Apparently the "not-for-profit" type of organization has appealed to many people as a happy compromise possessing many of the advantages of a cooperative but avoiding many of the problems. The objectives of nonprofit day care can be posed in terms of good care for children, subject to a financial viability constraint, and parents and other interested or expert parties can be given considerable direct access to policy decisions and operations. Since nonprofits are organized around a paid cadre of decisionmakers and workers, the instability and cumbersomeness of pure cooperative organizations can be avoided. Such a regime avoids the monopoly that almost seems inherent in public provision and permits consumer choice among alternative centers to carry greater weight in the evaluation machinery. These considerations have been key in explaining why the overwhelming majority of subsidized day care centers have been nonprofits.

How to Organize Day Care

The basic problems of organization seem to be these. First, well-informed consumer choice cannot be blythly assumed; some kind of special structure needs to be developed either to make consumer choice better informed or suppliers more concerned with the well-being of children, or both. Second, to the extent that market-like allocation mechanisms are weak, something must be put in place to assure that resources flow to where there are unmet demands.

The Fish Bowl, Parental Voice and Exit, and Regulation as Modes of Quality Control

The case against arch-type consumer choice—free enterprise in day care, i.e., the dangers of profit-taking at the expense of quality, seems persuasive to us. This view notwithstanding, however, there has been a surge of interest of profitmaking corporations in getting into the day care business. The profitmaking entities here are not the same as the small-scale independent proprietors currently providing (generally) low-cost day care but, rather, are companies proposing to design and set up a number of day care centers, perhaps operating them on a concession basis or as a kind of chain system. The corporations are suggesting that they can achieve significant economies of scale and greater efficiency in problem-solving ability than the standard not-for-profit organizations.[12] It is not clear whether these assertions are true or untrue. What does seem clear is that public policy should be wary of supporting the development of day care centers which are run primarily to make profits.

The nonprofit legal form appears to provide some protection, since the objectives of such organizations can be posed directly in terms of service to children rather than financial gain. However, while the not-for-profit legal form seems helpful in assuring trust-worthy day care centers, it certainly is not foolproof. (In fact, directors of nonprofit centers can be as selfish and neglectful of children in their pursuit of power and status as their profit-seeking counterparts.) Neither is the not-for-profit organizational form abso-lutely necessary. What *is* most important is that day care centers be open to detailed observation by both parents and citizen groups. Day care centers must operate in a *fish bowl*, which private enterprise generally has been reluctant to do.

The fish bowl environment is important for providing easier parental overview and influence—to gain some of the advantages of a cooperative. While informed choice can be made effective through exit as well as voice, where quality is hard to judge and where there is a mutual learning process on the part of supplier and demander regarding what is wanted and what can be done, control through exit or threat of exit is costly. And in child care there is reason to believe that too much shifting is detrimental to the child.

The fish bowl mechanism is not without problems, of course. Parents of preschoolers, especially parents who work or who are ill-educated, may be reluctant to involve themselves in day care operations, spend the time to see what is going on, or have the knowledge to evaluate what they see. There are possible avenues for overcoming these barriers, such as programs to educate parents, or having employers allow mothers time off for occasional visits to their children's day care centers. Yet even without such arrangements, it would appear that as long as parent overview is encouraged, indeed required, that *some* parents, or other involved citizens, would take the time to observe and participate.

Despite Hirschman's warning that a little exit can reduce the power of voice, and in spite of the costliness of exit in the day care context, it still seems desirable in the regime of day care to maintain the *option* of parental choice. Given parental choice we see no particular objection to providing day care by public agencies, as part of the system. The regime of subsidized day care should not have the habit of assigning children or families to particular facilities as appears to be common practice today. Parents will be drawn naturally to placing their children in the arrangement most convenient to them, but they should have a range of choice and good access to information about the alternatives.

If consumer choice is to be efficacious, however, consumers must be reasonably well informed about the alternatives. They need to know: How are different day care centers treating their children? What are high cost centers providing that the low cost centers are not? How worthwhile are these additional components in the eyes of child care experts and in the eyes of the parents? Providing such information will help to enable well-informed parental judgments. Given that parents are often uninformed, scrutiny of the services provided by individual suppliers and publicity of their evaluation may have a significant effect toward raising the quality of services.

The required information can be generated both formally and informally. Organizations providing day care, especially those receiving public subsidy funds, can be required to open their programs to informal parent and citizen review and observation. More systematic information can also be generated. A system of accreditation or ratings by some independent professional or philanthropic agency is one possibility, under which voluntary standards would be set up to guide consumer and supplier decisions. Another option is to initiate ongoing formal evaluation studies, carried out under the auspices of an official agency.[13] The day care sector must of course be properly organized to use this information effectively for evaluation purposes. Parents must have a choice of day care arrangements for their children. Parents and citizens must be able to participate in policy-making councils associated with individual day care arrangements *and* with agencies at the community level. With day care so structured, information provides the fuel for a viable evaluative process for governing the quality of care.

"Open" arrangements which operate to enable parental observation and influence and permit consumer choice seem to be the key to effective public control of day care. However, it seems necessary to supplement parental overview and choice with limited formal regulation. Certain regulations and funding standards can be set and should be enforced. However, it seems unwise to rest too much weight on formal regulatory machinery. Present formal regulation of day care centers for the most part consists of setting center requirements and seeing that centers meet a checklist of fire and building safety standards, pass a health inspection, meet certain staffing ratios, etc.

Formal regulatory authorities generally cannot spend much time overseeing each particular center, and generally are forced to use formal standards rather than judgments in regulating. To some extent, this may be attributable to the fact that it is easier and quicker to check a few conditions and numbers than to gain a reliable impression. But more importantly, the official power of the regulatory authority of necessity tends against judgment and towards rules. In the case of licensing regulations in particular (and perhaps for funding standards also), the use of judgment leads to an erratically enforced system which is open to litigation on grounds of (lack of) equity. Standards that are open to varying interpretation leave the door open to uneven protection of children, according to the whim of the various licensing inspectors, and lead to resentment on the part of licensees. Legal trends favor highly specific requirements which can be reasonably enforced, but this means that less tangible aspects of day care services cannot be easily regulated.[14] On the other hand, parents *may judge* (without formal documentation) that the center provides inferior services and withdraw their children. The center may try to persuade them otherwise, but the parents' act clearly is legitimate.

In this light it is useful to return to an earlier question: what should be the form of subsidy to day care? The clear implication of our discussion here is that subsidy should be implemented through a voucher-type system. There is no need that parents actually handle "pieces of paper" in the form of voucher certificates. What is important is that subsidy facilitates consumer choice by its attachment to children and not particular centers. Thus when a day care center admits a child, it knows that a subsidy check will be forthcoming, and when it loses a child it loses the corresponding subsidy.

It is something else when an arm of government (rather than a consumer) directly withdraws funding or a license to operate. Here due process requires more than the personal judgment of an inspector. Some specific code or standard must be violated. Thus, while traditional regulation can guard certain minimal regulations of health, safety, and enforce certain standards for space, staffing, and setting, etc., it cannot accomplish what some advocates expect from it, namely assuring the quality of program content and treatment of children. Such objectives are better addressed through parental overview and choice, and the provision of improved information to increase the effectiveness of these mechanisms.

Central Coordination and Supply Adjustment

A system based on improved information, consumer choice, parental overview, and hence suppliers not especially motivated by financial gain would appear to be capable of reasonable day care evaluation. Such a regime cannot be expected to have the same supply adjustment capability as traditional private enterprise, however. When demand expands for the services of a nonprofit center or a proprietary organization that is not aggressive after profits, what mechanisms induce its expansion? If it does not expand, what induces new entry at an appropriate location? While a regime of nonprofits with total revenue keyed to the number of children avoids much of the downward inflexibility associated with provision through a public bureaucracy, one would suspect sluggishness in expansion to meet new needs. Interviews with center directors and people responsible for overall day care organization in Washington, D.C., reinforce these suspicions.[15] Center directors seem prone to meet excess demand by enlarging the waiting list rather than by enlarging the facility. Establishment of new centers in areas of excess demand appears dependent on hard work of public-spirited citizens.

These considerations lead to two principal conclusions. First, in moving toward greater dependence on nonprofit-oriented suppliers, one should be wary of completely stamping out profitmaking day care enterprises. The flexibility that such a source of supply provides, at least over a period of transition, is not to be disregarded. Second, in a regime of nonprofit-oriented supply institutions there needs to be some kind of overall planning body that is responsible for assessing day care needs and has some power to allocate day care funds, particularly for the establishment of new centers. In what neighborhoods are there large unmet demands for day care? What hours do parents want day care? What components of day care do they consider most important and what are they willing to pay? Obtaining reasonable answers to these questions would be useful even if day care were provided largely through unregulated private enterprise. Having some official agency responsible for gaining answers to those questions and using this information to stimulate and coordinate supply adjustment is *essential* in a nonprofit-oriented regime. However, for such an agency to succeed in this mission it will need strong leverage over day care supply, as well as knowledge of the foregoing information. This leverage can be provided in the form of control over the allocation of capital funds for new day care facilities, and authority to designate which day care facilities are eligible to receive operating subsidies (vouchers) for serving preschool children.

Conclusion

In summary, public subsidy and organization policy for day care should focus on the objectives of maintaining and improving the quality of care for young children, accepting the economic facts of life that families will continue to demand these services, probably in increasing quantities even in the absence of public intervention. Such policy requires subsidies and complementary quality standards that foster competent, but not extravagant care, made widely available to all children whose parents need or choose to use it. Subsidies and fee schedules should be keyed to family incomes in order to neutralize the income barrier to the demand for good day care services. All young children, regardless of family status, should be eligible but not required to participate.

The evaluation and supply adjustment functions of the local day care sector require the development of better information through informal parent and citizen observation and formal systematic studies. Corresponding organizational arrangements are necessary to ensure that this information is generated and used effectively. Consumer choice, (parental choice among alternative day care programs) and parent and citizen participation in policymaking are required. A community planning body, capable of systematic study of day care quality and local day care needs, and able to use such information to plan and adjust day care supply through control of public subsidy funds, is also necessary.

Significant parts of what we are suggesting here have precedents in existing arrangements and proposed legislation. For example, we have suggested the need for a community planning organization to take comprehensive responsibility for local day care. Such a mandate is not very different from the objectives of the newly organized day care offices within the Department of Human Resources in Washington, D.C., or the functions envisioned for the local government "prime sponsors" under recently considered federal child development legislation (see Chapter 6). Nor is the mandate dissimilar to the objectives of the 4-C programs now operating in many local communities around the country.

The 4-C program and the child development legislation also emphasize another of our policy requirements—that of parent and citizen overview and participation in policymaking. The legislation, for example, provides for parent advisory groups for individual day care programs (Project Policy Committees) and parent and citizen councils (Child and Family Service Councils) attached to the local government prime sponsor agencies. The structures of 4-C agencies, on the other hand, are also intended to be broadly representative of parents and other day care interests in the community.

While the child development legislation has not left the drawing boards, and agencies of local government and 4-C programs are not currently in position to acquire the necessary leverage, it seems worthwhile noting that these elements could serve as basic building blocks to constructing a reformed day care system. The exact design of such a system remains to be worked out. On the surface at least it would seem desirable to have a single agency in the local executive branch of government administer the executive functions of licensing and inspection, distribution of public subsidy funds, systematic data collection and analysis of day care needs and resources, and planning of day care supply on a communitywide basis. On the other hand, an agency like 4-C would usefully serve, in its representative capacity, to informally monitor and evaluate local day care arrangements, bring together local child care interests, and develop and approve the general policy used by the executive agency for regulating and allocating resources to local day care. Such a system is like that envisioned in the proposed federal child development legislation wherein the local government prime sponsor agency would serve to administer public support of local day care, subject to the policymaking approval of the Child and Family Service Councils. We are not suggesting that 4-C, as currently constituted, is perfectly structured to take on the role of this council, although one special strength of 4-C is that it represents a variety of child care interests and would provide necessary scope to the development and coordination of day care policy in the context of multiple public programs related to children. Nor are present executive agencies of general local government perfectly suited for comprehensive administration of local day care. But it does seem desirable that any reform of the day care system build on these existing institutions and the work some of them have already accomplished. The objective of organizational reform should be to mold these elements into an arrangement where they work with, rather than at cross-purposes to one another.

5

Planning and Evaluation of Day Care at the Community Level

Richard Zamoff and
Jerolyn Lyle

Introduction

Our analysis thus far emphasizes community planning, parent and citizen participation, and consumer choice for dealing with the supply-adjustment and evaluation problems of day care. These concepts would be embodied in an organizational arrangement featuring a community planning body responsible for coordinating public and private day care resources, facilitating licensing procedures, enforcing day care regulations and standards, allocating public funds, and setting priorities for new day care projects. This agency would be complemented by parent-citizen councils to oversee resource allocation policy and help evaluate operating day care arrangements. To carry out its own responsibilities and to enhance the viability of citizen participation and consumer choice, the community planning agency must develop systematic and detailed information about the preferences and satisfaction of day care users, and the nature of the supply and demand for local day care arrangements. Without effective means for obtaining and interpreting such information, the evaluation mechanisms of participation and choice will be weakened, and machinery for planning and coordination of day care supply will fail.

It is the purpose of this chapter, therefore, to illustrate how information can be developed in a way that is within the capabilities of local agencies and how that information is useful for regulating and planning local day care. The "assessment" methodology that we present was developed at the Urban Institute and field tested in three neighborhoods in Washington, D.C. The data from one neighbor-

This chapter is based on materials in Richard B. Zamoff and Jerolyn R. Lyle, "Assessment of Day Care Services and Needs at the Community Level: Mt. Pleasant," Urban Institute Paper 714-1-1, November 1971.

hood, Mt. Pleasant, are illustrated here to show the kinds of information that can be collected and how this information relates to planning and regulatory decisions.

The procedures for collecting data can be carried out by volunteer workers. The requirements for analyzing the data are within the current expertise of many local government agencies, and certainly within the potential capability of most local agencies that might serve in the capacity of a community planning body. A small group of professional analysts was necessary in the test demonstrations to help organize and design the assessment efforts. However, even this requirement is small, and would become less important as the methodology became routine and widespread. Thus, the method which we discuss seems a reasonable prototype for use by local agencies responsible for day care.[1]

Information Requirements

The information required for planning and regulatory decisions on local day care includes measures of various aspects of demand, supply, and performance. In particular, several categories of data need to be developed.

First, the dimensions of demand for day care in the community must be determined. "Target" clientele groups for day care must be described by standard demographic variables, sizes, and locations. This information, in conjunction with estimates of the existing supply of day care arrangements, provides guidance as to where day care capacity should be expanded and where it might be contracted.

For effective planning the community agency also needs information about the nature and strength of preferences of target clientele for day care programs of different kinds. In particular, it is important to assess parents' preferences and willingness to pay for different types of day care programs and to determine what specific (packages of) services are preferred (e.g., transportation, food, flexible time scheduling, etc.). Such information is helpful for developing priorities for allocating resources among different types of programs, and for predicting how heavily new arrangements will be patronized and how satisfied prospective users are likely to be.

Furthermore, and of crucial importance, information on target populations and the kinds of day care they deem important assists (within limits of minimum acceptability) in determining reasonable standards for funding local day care. For as we have noted earlier, raising the standards for day care will limit the proportion of potential clientele that can be served within existing resource constraints. Measurement of the size of target groups makes this "quality-quantity trade-off" explicit to day care planners.

Second, the community agency must also measure various aspects of the supply of local day care. Specifically, it must find out what type of day care arrangements are currently provided, who uses them, and what they cost. This information describes the base on which expanded or modified day care services for the community must be built. The community agency can begin to develop its priorities for planning and allocating resources by comparing the nature of demand (dimensions and preferences of target groups) with the nature of the current supply.

Third, the community agency must determine what resources are available in the community for supporting programs which address its priorities. In particular, information must be obtained on what parents (in different income groups) are willing to pay for different kinds of day care arrangements, and what other community resources, such as volunteer labor and capital facilities, are available for day care. These data are essential for determining policy for subsidy and fee schedules for day care services and, given the availability of public funds, for evaluating the quantity/quality trade-off.

Taken together, the information on target groups, and their preferences, existing supply, and local resources form the basis for rational planning and allocation decisions. In addition to this information the community agency will want to monitor community residents' satisfaction with current programs in order to adjust its priorities among types of programs and provide information for the evaluation decisions of parent-consumers and citizen-participants on policy councils.

The Methodology

Certain basic data are available from the census and other official sources. In particular, a community planning agency might well be interested in the following items available on a census tract, service area, or citywide basis:[2] percentage of dwelling units with children under age six, percentage of children enrolled in kindergarten, median family income, percentage of population under six years of age, percentage of households headed by a single (including divorced, separated, or widowed) male or female, percentage of married women in labor force with husband present, and percentage of married women in labor force with children under age six.[3] These types of data are directly useful not only for decisionmaking purposes, but also for verifying the representativeness of the sample that is constructed for the community telephone survey, which we shall discuss below.

Several kinds of survey instruments are useful for collecting information to augment census data, including on-site interviews with day care suppliers and day care users.[4] However, our discussion here focuses mainly on the use of a telephone survey to interview randomly selected community residents. The telephone survey involves a sequence of steps. First, a random sample of households in the community is selected with the aid of a reverse telephone directory, i.e., a directory which lists telephone numbers alphabetically according to street address, thus making it easy to identify all telephone listings in a given geographic area. These directories are available for a fee from local telephone companies. While households listed in the phone directory are not exactly representative of households in the community at large, experience in Washington, D.C., suggests that the distortions are not very important (by most demographic or socioeconomic variables of interest).[5] Thus, a random sample drawn from such a directory may be expected to be roughly representative of the community. Furthermore, any population subgroup (such as households with children) extracted from the directory sample can be expected to be approximately representative of that subgroup in the population at large. Thus the telephone directory sampling strategy is useful for selecting a representative sample of current and potential day care users in the community. Such an approach is preferable to such other possible strategies as sampling from lists supplied by day care centers or day care homes, for the latter are not likely to produce representative samples. For example, households whose children have dropped out of a day care center or whose parents are most dissatisfied with aspects of a center's care are not likely to be included in a list supplied by those operating day care arrangements.

To establish a representative sample of households useful for analysis of local day care, short screening interviews are conducted by phone to identify those households in the original sample with at least one child under six years of age. Other age ranges may also be specified or other variables (such as parents' employment status) may be designated for screening purposes as well. Screening on too many variables must be avoided, however, for screening interviews must be kept to only a few minutes, since respondents, having had no warning that they would be called, may not find it convenient to talk at length.

Households which have been screened by the desired variables, and which express willingness to cooperate, will be called later for the more extensive "primary" interviews. Thus, one of the functions of the screening interviews is to determine whether respondents are willing to be interviewed at all, and if so, what time of day is convenient for them, and whether they prefer to be interviewed in English or Spanish (or presumably other languages if the interviewing capability is available).[6]

Once the screening interviews are completed, and the original sample reduced to households of interest (e.g., those having at least one child under the age of six), letters are sent to these screened sample households, informing them of the extended telephone interviews that will follow. The letter describes the purpose of the survey, assures anonymity of responses, and solicits cooperation.

Finally, the primary telephone interviews are administered to the screened sample of households. The interview questions are designed to gather detailed information on respondents, including socioeconomic data. Only after these interviews have been completed can the statistical "adequacy" of the screened sample really be determined. The adequacy of this sample is measured in two dimensions: whether households in the sample are typical, demographically and socioeconomically, of the subpopulation they represent in the community at large; and secondly, whether particular subsamples within the overall screened sample, e.g., users of day care homes, are represented in sufficient numbers to effect meaningful analyses and comparisons with other subsamples. The problem of representativeness can be checked to some extent by comparing the detailed interview information with information available from census and other official sources. The adequacy of subsample sizes can be checked directly by tabulating the interview data. If the sample has yielded particular subsamples that are not large enough for meaningful comparisons, then the process of sampling, screening, and interviewing must be continued to enlarge the screened sample until subsamples are built up to the desired levels.

In the study we shall shortly report, the primary telephone interview was the basic source of information for analysis and planning of local day care requirements. This interview included a variety of questions about the structure and income of the household, preference and usage of different types of day care arrangements, willingness to pay for various services, and other subjects. The interview consisted of both "closed" and "open-ended" questions and took approximately thirty minutes to administer.[7]

Experience has shown that a telephone interview can be used to good advantage, producing data which would be at least as good as and in some instances superior to that obtained by personal interviews. The proportions of "no answer" and "don't know" responses are comparable, and the length of answers are about the same. In short, there should be very little loss of information using telephone interviewing procedures providing they are properly executed, supervised, and controlled.

In addition, compared to the personal interview, the telephone interview has other practical advantages.[8] It eliminates travel and substantially reduces costs. When no one answers, call-backs are not only feasible, but can be made at virtually all hours of the day. If calls are made from a central location, they can be monitored and faulty interviewing procedures corrected on the spot.

Illustrated Use of the Assessment Method

In this section we present some results of the telephone survey in the Mt. Pleasant neighborhood of Wasington, D.C. This illustration is not intended as a detailed blueprint for how collected data should be processed for decision purposes. Such an objective is beyond the scope of this volume. Rather, the example provides a general idea of the types of data that can be obtained and how such data can be interpreted for planning and evaluation purposes. In doing this we believe we are presenting realistic support for the contention that a well-prepared community planning agency can economically develop the information needed to successfully carry out its responsibilities toward planning and regulating local day care.

To provide some perspective on the Mt. Pleasant neighborhood, the following data were readily obtained from the census, supplemented by the telephone interviews with a screened survey sample consisting of parents in 211 households representing approximately 35 percent of the children below age six living in the geographic study area: Mt. Pleasant residents are 65 percent black, with concentrations of whites increasing with age. The median age of residents is 29.5 years, and children under six represent 8.7 percent of the population. The area is relatively stable, with one-fourth of the respondents to the survey having lived at their present addresses for over six years. The great majority of households are headed by men (69.2 percent). Of those interviewed families headed by women, virtually all are single-parent households.

Demands

One can try to assess the (potential) demand for day care in various ways. First, one is interested in the one-parent households, which can be expected to be especially heavy demanders. Table 5-1 displays the percentage of surveyed households in Mt. Pleasant without mothers, and without fathers, by income classification. Not unexpectedly,

Table 5-1
Households Without Mothers and Fathers as Percentage of All Households, by Income of Household (N=211)[a]

Average Weekly Household Income Per Capita		Households Without Mothers, as Percentage of All Households	Households Without Fathers, as Percentage of All Households
$ 0-$14	(N=48)	6.0	60.0
$15-$29	(N=68)	3.0	40.0
$30-$44	(N=29)	0.0	3.0
$45-$59	(N=25)	0.0	16.0
$60-$74	(N=22)	0.0	5.0
$75 and over	(N=19)	0.0	11.0

[a]Totals do not equal 100.0% given column and row headings. The *N* values in parentheses represent the sample sizes in each income class.

these households are found to be disproportionately poor, indicating that the heaviest users of day care are also likely to be the most in need of public support if the day care they choose is to be of good quality.

A second way of assessing day care demand is to consider households with working mothers. Ninety-eight of the 211 sampled households had working mothers, and were highly dependent on the mother's income, as Table 5-2 suggests. Again it is the poor households in this category that will be the heaviest users, and these will require significant subsidy to assure adequate quality of care.

A third way of assessing demand is to ask both unemployed and employed mothers whether they would work, or work more hours, if satisfactory day care arrangements were available. Sixty-four percent of the 136 households in our subsample in which mothers were not working full time fit this description. Furthermore, the percentage of mothers in this category was found to vary significantly with the mothers' occupation, as Table 5-3 attests. The additional time that children of these mothers would spend in extra-family day care, if suitable arrangements were available, constitute an important measure of potential demand. Finally, one can pose the question of latent demand for day care by assessing the degree to which mothers who currently do not use extra-family day care would consider leaving their children in such care if satisfactory arrangements were available to them. Table 5-4 indicates how this subsample of 163 households would respond to the possibility of having alternative types of extra-family day care facilities made available to them.

Table 5-2

Average Proportion of Total Weekly Household Income Earned by Mothers for Households with Working Mothers, by Income of Household (N=98)[a]

Average Weekly Household Income Per Capita	%
$ 0-$14	100.0
$15-$29	67.0
$30-$44	54.0
$45-$59	60.0
$60-$74	55.0
$75 and over	63.0

[a]Total does not equal 100.0% given column and row headings.

Table 5-3

Mothers Who Would Work (Work More Hours) If Satisfactory Day Care Was Available as Proportion of All Mothers Not Working Full Time, by Occupation of Mother (N=136)[a]

Occupation of Mother	%
Housewife or retired	71.0
Professional, managerial	42.0
Sales, clerical, technical	80.0
Crafts	75.0
Operatives, laborers	36.0
Service Workers	82.0

[a]Total does not equal 100.0% given column and row headings.

Table 5-5 gives some perspective on the distribution of preferences relative to a few dimensions of day care programs. Mothers in Mt. Pleasant indicated particular interest in arrangements that would allow them to leave a child for only a few hours to go shopping, look for a job, or attend to other personal business. The interest in day care varied considerably with the ages of preschool children, and Table 5-6 shows that the type of arrangements desired also varies with children's ages. Informal arrangements (home-like settings) were more preferred for infants and toddlers, while the more formal arrangements (day care centers) were more popular for preschoolers in the three to six year age range. This is not surprising since informal

Table 5-4

Respondents Who Would Consider Leaving Children in Day Care Center, Family Day Care Home, or Group Day Care Home If Such Arrangement Was Available[a]

Arrangement	%
Day Care Center	51.5
Family Day Care Home	45.4
Group Day Care Home	26.4
Would not consider day care center, family day care home, or group day care home	8.6
Total Respondents	163

[a]Based upon answers of 163 respondents to whom such a day care arrangement is not currently available. Responses exceed 100.0% because some respondents indicated they would consider leaving their children in more than one type of day care arrangement.

80

Table 5-5

Proportion of Respondents Indicating Great Interest in Various Types of Day Care Arrangements by Income of Household (N=211)[a]

Arrangement	Average Weekly Household Income Per Capita						All Income Classes
	$0-$14 (N=48)	$15-$29 (N=68)	$30-$44 (N=29)	$45-$59 (N=25)	$60-$74 (N=22)	$75 and Over (N=19)	
Infant day care for children from birth to 3 years of age	35.0	44.0	41.0	44.0	55.0	37.0	41.7
Day care for children between ages 3 and 6	52.0	51.0	41.0	60.0	50.0	58.0	51.7
Day care starting at 6:00 A.M.	35.0	37.0	31.0	20.0	23.0	58.0	34.1
Day care until 9:00 P.M.	25.0	25.0	28.0	12.0	0.0	37.0	22.7
Day care on Saturdays and Sundays from 9:00 A.M. to 5:00 P.M.	13.0	7.0	28.0	0.0	0.0	11.0	10.0
24 hour day care	23.0	10.0	7.0	8.0	0.0	11.0	11.4
Day care where a parent can leave a child for a few hours while she goes to the doctor, looking for a job, shopping, or somewhere else	88.0	76.0	66.0	80.0	68.0	79.0	76.8
Babysitting for groups of about 30 children	13.0	4.0	10.0	16.0	18.0	21.0	11.8

[a]Total does not equal 100.0% given column and row headings.

Table 5-6

Day Care Arrangements Preferred for Children Under Age 3 and Between Ages 3 and 6[a]

Arrangement	Under 3 %	Between 3 and 6 %
Informal:		
Other member of household	16.3	24.6
Relative or friend from outside household	18.3	13.6
Hired sitter in own home	16.3	8.5
Hired sitter outside home	4.8	1.7
Formal:		
Family day care home	19.2	11.9
Group day care home	6.7	11.9
Day care center	18.3	28.0
Total Respondents	104	118

[a]Based upon answers provided by 104 respondents with children under age three, and 118 respondents with children between ages three and six, who would prefer to use some type of day care arrangement.

arrangements seem more likely to give children more individual attention in a home-like setting, conditions which seem more important for the younger child. Despite this preference pattern, however, only 8.6 percent of the respondents said they would not consider more formal day care arrangements for their younger children, if such arrangements were available in Mt. Pleasant. The great emphasis placed on staff competence by mothers in all income groups may account for the willingness of mothers to whom formal day care is not now available to consider it for the young child. The stress on staff competence is clearly illustrated by the data in Table 5-7, which demonstrates that respondents give it heavy emphasis over education, nutrition, recreation, and sanitation aspects of day care. However, more probing seems necessary to determine exactly what parents mean by competence, or how it would be recognized.

Available Supply

Table 5-8 summarizes the nature of arrangements respondents of the telephone survey said were available to them. And Table 5-9 shows

Table 5-7

Top Priorities of Respondents for Day Care Services for Children Under Age 3 and Between Ages 3 and 6 (N=211)

	Under 3 %	Between 3 and 6 %
Should have a competent staff	76.8	67.3
Should provide educational services	36.0	54.0
Should provide nutritional services	29.9	31.8
Should be clean	23.2	17.1
Should provide recreational facilities	18.0	19.9

Table 5-8

Day Care Arrangements Available to Respondents (N=211)

Available	Other Members of Household %	Relative or Friend from Outside Household %	Hired Sitter in Own Home or Hired Sitter Outside Home %	Family Day Care Home or Group Day Care Home %	Day Care Center %
Yes	43.6	43.1	37.9	16.6	14.2
No	56.4	53.1	56.4	76.8	77.7
Don't know	0.0	3.8	5.7	6.6	8.1

the kinds of arrangements actually utilized by day care users, for two age groups of children. (It is notable here that no respondents used a day care center at the time of the survey.)[9] Table 5-10 supplements the patronage information by describing the time usage pattern of existing day care arrangements. As shown, Mt. Pleasant parents tend to use day care arrangements either for less than 20 or more than 40 hours per week. These arrangements include relatives, friends, and neighbors, as well as family or group day care homes and day care centers. The time flexibility of these more informal modes of supply may account partially for their attractiveness to parents. Such data may serve to alert planners and suppliers of more formal day care center arrangements to this requirement.

Finally, in assessing the nature of current supply, one is most interested in the costs of day care arrangements. Table 5-11 indicates

Table 5-9
Day Care Arrangements Used for Children Under Age 3 and Between Ages 3 and 6 While Respondents Are Away From Home On a Regular Basis[a]

Arrangement	Under 3 %	Between 3 and 6 %
Other member of household	25.8	40.2
Relative or friend from outside household	31.5	28.0
Hired sitter in own home	13.5	12.2
Hired sitter outside home	20.2	11.0
Family day care home	6.7	6.1
Group day care home	2.2	2.4
Day care center	0.0	0.0
Total Respondents	89	82

[a]Based upon answers provided by 89 respondents with children under age three, and 82 respondents with children between ages three and six, who are using some type of day care arrangement.

Table 5-10
Number of Hours Children Under Age 3 and Between Ages 3 and 6 Are In Day Care Arrangements[a]

Number of Hours	Under 3 %	Between 3 and 6 %
1 hour-19 hours	34.8	42.7
20 hours-39 hours	22.4	18.3
40 hours and over	38.2	35.4
No answer	4.5	3.7
Total Respondents	89	82

[a]Based upon answers provided by 89 respondents with children under age three, and 82 respondents with children between ages three and six, who are using some type of day care arrangement.

what respondents to the survey are now paying for the arrangements which they use. The table shows that very large proportions of Mt. Pleasant residents use child care arrangements so informal that no monetary cost is involved. Of course, information on costs from telephone respondents only indicates how much users pay, and not the actual cost structure of day care programs. But payment information from users may be supplemented by financial statements from day care suppliers. In addition, interviews with day care

Table 5-11

Weekly Cost to Parents of Day Care Arrangements for Children Under Age 3 and Between Ages 3 and 6[a]

Cost	Under 3 %	Between 3 and 6 %
No cost	39.3	56.1
Under $10.00	6.7	8.5
$10.00-$15.99	20.2	8.5
$16.00-$21.99	11.2	13.4
$22.00-$27.99	7.9	1.2
$28.00 and over	10.1	9.8
No answer	4.5	2.4
Total Respondents	89	82

[a]Based upon answers provided by 89 respondents with children under age three, and 82 respondents with children between ages three and six, who are using some type of day care arrangement.

suppliers can help to obtain required data on costs and other aspects of particular day care centers or homes.[10] Nevertheless cost data may sometimes be very difficult to obtain from private operators and for informal day care arrangements. For example, some informal arrangements may involve no monetary transactions at all. Despite these difficulties, efforts must be made to obtain reliable information on costs and payments as these data are essential to planning and resource allocation decisions not only for the community planning body, but also for the individual day care users and suppliers.

Willingness to Pay and Community Resources

The supply and usage data become particularly important when measured against the preference patterns of users, for this type of comparison suggests priorities for new programs. Table 5-12 compares the usage and preference patterns among alternative types of day care arrangements obtained from respondents for two age groups of children. The disparities suggest that parents would like an expansion in the availability of formal organized day care facilities (centers and family and group homes) in the Mt. Pleasant neighborhood. However, the interview information also indicates that parents

Table 5-12

Comparison of Day Care Arrangements Used and Preferred for Children Under Age 3 and Between Ages 3 and 6[a]

Arrangement	Under 3		Between 3 and 6	
	Used %	Preferred %	Used %	Preferred %
Other member of household	25.8	16.3	40.2	24.6
Relative or friend from outside household	31.5	18.3	28.0	13.6
Hired sitter in own home	13.5	16.3	12.2	8.5
Hired sitter outside home	20.2	4.8	11.0	1.7
Family day care home	6.7	19.2	6.1	11.9
Group day care home	2.2	6.7	2.4	11.9
Day care center	0.0	18.3	0.0	28.0
Total Respondents	89	104	82	118

[a]Based upon answers provided by 89 respondents with children under age three, and 82 respondents with children between ages three and six, who are using some type of day care arrangement, and upon answers provided by 104 respondents with children under age three, and 118 respondents with children between ages three and six, who would prefer to use some type of day care arrangement.

are unlikely to be willing to pay the cost of child care at day care centers.

The data in Table 5-13 indicates what respondent mothers in Mt. Pleasant who were not working full time said they would be willing

Table 5-13

Average Weekly Cost Mothers Would be Willing to Pay for Day Care as Proportion of Expected Average Weekly Earnings by Income of Household, for Mothers Not Working Full Time (N=136)[a]

Average Weekly Household Income Per Capita	%
$ 0-$14	32.0
$15-$29	28.0
$30-$44	25.0
$45-$59	24.0
$60-$74	21.0
$75 and over	31.0

[a]Total does not equal 100.0% given column and row headings.

to pay for day care as a proportion of their incomes. We find that in all income classes these mothers would pay upwards of 20 percent of their incomes for child care. Women with lower earnings are willing to pay greater proportions of their income for child care, in cognizance of the higher costs of care relative to their incomes. It is noteworthy, however, that what parents are willing to pay generally falls well below what "quality day care" is believed to cost.

Not surprisingly, the willingness to pay for child care varies with the type of services offered. In Table 5-14 we see that the amounts Mt. Pleasant respondents were willing to pay generally increased with the formality of the day care arrangement. Table 5-15 provides some detail on the willingness to pay for basic care and various "component" services such as education, transportation, and nutrition for children in the three to six year age bracket. Here we see, for example, that in terms of willingness to pay, an additional "education component" was generally considered more important than flexible program hours or a more convenient opening or closing time. (It is not entirely clear, however, what parents have in mind by a preschool education program, i.e., formal emphasis on cognitive skills, or something more general.)

In addition to monetary resources, a community agency would want to know the extent to which labor and capital facilities were

Table 5-14

Weekly Cost Respondents Are Willing to Pay for Alternative Types of Day Care Arrangements (N=211)

Cost	Other Member of Household %	Relative or Friend from Outside Household %	Hired Sitter in Own Home or Hired Sitter Outside Home %	Family Day Care Home or Group Day Care Home %	Day Care Center %
No Cost	30.8	13.7	4.3	3.3	2.4
Under $10.00	0.0	1.9	0.9	0.9	0.9
$10.00-$15.99	2.8	9.0	13.7	5.2	1.9
$16.00-$21.99	3.3	6.6	5.7	2.8	2.8
$22.00-$27.99	0.0	0.9	2.8	0.0	1.4
$28.00 and over	2.4	4.3	16.1	4.7	2.4
Don't know	4.3	10.4	0.0	6.2	10.4
Not available	56.4	53.1	56.4	76.8	77.7

Table 5-15

Average Weekly Cost Parents Are Willing to Pay Per Child for Basic Day Care Program and for Additional Program Components by Income of Household, for Children Between Ages 3 and 6 (N=211)

Average Weekly Household Income Per Capita		Basic Day Care	Additional Program Component				
			Preschool Educational Program	Transportation	One Hot Meal	Open Until 9:00 P.M.	Open on Weekends
$ 0-$14	(N=48)	$11.98	$ 8.14	$4.45	$3.43	$1.30	$1.00
$15-$29	(N=68)	11.74	5.91	3.73	3.40	0.50	0.83
$30-$44	(N=29)	11.36	9.75	5.28	4.08	3.64	1.78
$45-$59	(N=25)	15.50	9.65	4.95	4.39	1.26	2.60
$60-$74	(N=22)	8.95	10.25	5.65	4.27	1.45	1.63
$75 and over	(N=19)	15.44	8.05	4.68	4.26	3.27	3.11
All Income Classes	(N=211)	12.23	8.03	4.53	3.78	1.55	1.49

88

available to support day care in the community. The survey in Mt. Pleasant revealed, for example, that over half of the respondents were interested in establishing day care arrangements in their own homes, while other respondents indicated willingness to contribute their time in helping to run day care programs, participate in policymaking, and evaluate and inspect programs and facilities. No information was collected on the monetary compensation expected (if any) in return for these contributions.

Evaluation of Day Care Arrangements

The telephone survey ascertained reasons why respondents did not want to use particular types of day care arrangements and why certain respondents removed their children from day care programs. The results are illustrated in Tables 5-16 and 5-17. Here, while the large majority of respondents offered no criticisms, some did provide

Table 5-16

Reasons Respondents Would Not Want to Use Different Types of Day Care Arrangements (N=211)[a]

Arrangement	Reason(s)
Other members of household	Don't like others caring for children (4.7) No objection to arrangement (94.3)
Relative or friend from outside household	Don't like others caring for children (9.0) Better care elsewhere (5.2) No objection to arrangement (91.0)
Hired sitter in own home or hired sitter outside home	Don't like others caring for children (15.2) Better care elsewhere (9.0) Too expensive (5.7) No objection to arrangement (81.5)
Family day care home or group day care home	Better care elsewhere (8.5) Don't like others caring for children (8.1) Too expensive (7.1) Overcrowded (6.2) No objection to arrangement (72.5)
Day care center	Don't like others caring for children (9.0) Better care elsewhere (5.7) Too expensive (4.7) No objection to arrangement (81.5)

[a]The percentages in parentheses indicate the proportion of respondents providing the reason listed.

Table 5-17
Reasons for Removal of Children from Day Care Arrangement (N=31)[a]

Reason(s)	%
Didn't like care given to child	38.7
Mother stopped working	29.0
Child disliked arrangements	19.4
Too expensive	12.9
Child wasn't developing	12.9
Child became ineligible because of age	6.5
Mother found more satisfactory arrangement	6.5
Child went to kindergarten	3.2
Child became ill	3.2

[a]Based upon answers of 31 respondents who have removed children from day care arrangements. Responses exceed 100.0% because some respondents provided more than one reason for removing a child from a day care arrangement.

reasons for their dissatisfaction. The reasons given by 31 respondents who withdrew children from day care arrangements related largely to the parent's or child's perception of the quality of care, lending credence to consumer choice (and parent overview) as operative mechanisms of evaluation.

The information in Tables 5-16 and 5-17 is aggregated over users of several different day care arrangements. In this form, the information on user satisfaction, in conjunction with other data, can be used to discern what hazards are associated with given types of arrangements, and what types of arrangements most consistently produce satisfactory results. Such information is of clear relevance for establishing planning and allocation policy. But information on user satisfaction can just as easily be collected and tabulated for users of (selected) individual day care facilities. Collection and publicity of such information on this basis, would serve to educate parent-consumers in their decisions to patronize particular facilities. In addition, such information would serve to alert day care officials and policymakers to arrangements which seem not to be performing satisfactorily. Parent councils, and the community planning body, could follow-up this information with further investigations. Ultimately these organizational units could bring pressures to bear on suppliers, through funding and licensing decisions and other means, to stimulate corrective actions.

Conclusion

This chapter has illustrated how a formal assessment methodology, centered around a telephone sample survey, may be used by a community agency to obtain certain kinds of information crucial to successful planning and regulation of local day care. The method is used to develop information about the demand for day care, the day care preferences of users and potential users, the extent, usage, and cost of the current supply of day care arrangements, the discrepancies between current supply and needs and preferences of target groups, the community resources available for supporting local day care, and community satisfaction with ongoing day care operations. This information facilitates successful oversight, planning, and regulation of local day care, and is obtained in a manner well within the analytical and other resource capabilities of local agencies. Hence, the approach can serve as a prototype for adoption in most communities.

As noted earlier, the concepts of community planning, consumer choice, and parent and citizen participation seem essential to successful day care sector operation. But good information is required for such machinery to function properly. Furthermore, the use of formal assessment methods of the kind illustrated in this chapter is necessary for providing a major component of the required data. Without such information, the evaluation mechanisms of parent participation and consumer choice will be less effective. And without systematic information, central community planning will certainly be frustrated in dealing with the supply adjustment problems that plague the day care sector.

6

National Day Care Policy

Richard Nelson and Dennis Young

Introduction

In this final chapter we will summarize and extend what we believe are the important implications of our analysis for an evolving national day care policy. The focus of the discussion will be the Comprehensive Headstart, Child Development, and Family Service Act (referred to here as the Child Development Act).[1] While the fate of that particular act may not be bright, future day care legislation undoubtedly will and should be based on the groundwork that it provides. It seems useful, therefore, to conclude this volume by discussing the act's strengths and weaknesses.

The Purpose of a National Day Care Policy

The Child Development Act is only one of a number of pieces of legislation affecting day care that have recently come before Congress. It is important to distinguish this legislation from the others, both in purpose and in substance.

The Family Assistance Plan is another important piece of proposed legislation which includes a significant extension of day care. Under this program, day care is supported for the purpose of taking care of children of poor families with training or working mothers. The principal objective of the legislation is to raise the incomes of the poor in such a way as to keep welfare costs low. The proposed solution is to get welfare mothers to work, but it is recognized that if mothers are to work someone must care for their children. However, concern for the welfare and development of children is almost ignored by the welfare legislation.

Thus, the arguments for public support of day care under the Family Assistance Plan are quite different from the articulated purposes of the Child Development Act. The latter is rooted in the Headstart experience and is aimed at helping children whether or not their parents are away from home during the day. Enabling mothers to work is incidental to the discussion of day care under this legislation. Rather, the day care is seen as a means of providing the child with better care and enriching his intellectual experiences and socialization process. Another aspect which differentiates the child development legislation is its inclusion of middle- and upper-income families as potential clientele. This wider orientation supports the view that developmental day care may be advantageous to all children, rich and poor alike, and in this sense is consistent with our national educational policies for older children.

The tension between the welfare-oriented and child-focused sources of support for day care leads to serious policy conflicts. For example, various studies have shown that for poor, not well-educated mothers with two or more young children, the costs of "adequate" care will be nearly as great as (and perhaps greater than) her expected salary.[2] In the absence of subsidy of day care she will not use such expensive care if she chooses to work. If there is to be subsidy of day care with a cut-off point at a relatively low income level then there exists a perverse incentive for mothers either to keep the income that they earn low, or to use cheaper day care. If incentives to work or to use day care of good quality are to be preserved over a wide range of income levels, then partial subsidy of day care must extend up into moderate income ranges and the fiscal costs of day care become very large. Awareness of the high welfare program costs of a graduated subsidy program creates pressures on government to *force* mothers to work so as to preserve the viability of a subsidy cut-off, and to somehow force down the costs of day care. Since benefits for children are more or less incidental to the foregoing welfare policy dialogue, it is apparent that children would bear the brunt of cost cutting. Thus, day care keyed to the objective of getting mothers of young children out into the labor force is in danger of making everyone worse off: (the taxpayers), because even with strong downward pressure on costs subsidizing day care is an inefficient way of subsidizing incomes, the mother forced away from her children and into a job that she does not like, and of particular importance, the children themselves.

It seems far more sensible to view public support of day care as a service for children of poor families or for children in general. For this reason our sympathies lie with the child development day care legislation.

The Comprehensive Headstart, Child Development, and Family Services Act

This proposed legislation authorizes funds and specifies an administrative structure for providing a variety of services related to the care and development of children, up to age fifteen. All children are eligible for services, but priority is given to preschool, economically disadvantaged children, children of working mothers and single parents, and migrant and Indian children.

The program would be administered by the U.S. Department of Health, Education and Welfare, Office of Child Development, through a set of prime sponsors in local areas. These prime sponsors would contract with various public and private agencies for the provision of child care "projects," or may provide some of these projects themselves. The prime sponsors would be selected by the Secretary of HEW based on certain qualifications, and the submission of program statements. Prime sponsors would normally be units or combinations of units of local government, representing populations of 25,000 or more. For localities unrepresented by a qualifying local prime sponsor applicant, the state may be designated to serve as prime sponsor, with additional requirements for local representation (discussed below). The chief executive of the prime sponsor government may designate the particular agency, i.e., government department or nonprofit corporation, to administer the program.

Each prime sponsor must establish a Child and Family Service Council whose purpose is to approve the program statements, goals, policies, and procedures of the prime sponsor, and the selection and renewal of projects funded by the prime sponsor. The council must also provide for evaluation of programs which the prime sponsor supports. If the prime sponsor is a state, then it must, in addition, designate local family service areas of under 50,000 in population and establish local program councils for each of these areas. A local program council is authorized to approve the program statements of the state and projects authorized in its own local area.

The Child and Family Service Councils are to be composed of ten members, at least half of whom are parents of children served by projects supported by the act. These parent members are to be chosen by local program councils if the prime sponsor is a state, or otherwise by Headstart and other Project Policy Committees associated with individual projects funded by the prime sponsor. The remaining members of the Child and Family Service Councils are appointed by the chief executive officer of the prime sponsor; half of those appointed members are to be "broadly representative of the public" and the other half knowledgeable in child care disciplines. One-third of the membership of the councils is required to be economically disadvantaged.

Individual child care projects are to be provided either directly by the prime sponsor, or by subcontracting with public or private agencies. In the latter case, potential provider agencies are to submit project applications to the prime sponsor. Individual projects must establish project policy committees responsible for approving the basic goals of the projects and for planning, monitoring, and evaluating their performance. These committees are also to be composed at least half of parents with children served by the projects; the remainder are persons representative of the community and at least one member skilled in a child care discipline. In the event that the prime sponsor provides projects of its own, the plans for these projects must be submitted and approved directly by the Secretary of HEW.

The program statements submitted to HEW by prime sponsors are supposed to include provisions for coordination with prime sponsors in neighboring areas, coordination with other social programs such as employment and manpower, coordination with local educational agencies to provide for continuity with elementary school programs, regular dissemination of information to parents in the community, and plans for conducting regular surveys and analyses of needs for child development and family services in the prime sponsor area. The prime sponsors are to give "special consideration" to project applications by public and private *nonprofit* agencies.

Program financing is to be made through a fixed annual appropriation by Congress apportioned among states and localities by a formula involving the number of disadvantaged children, children under age six, and children of working mothers and single parents in the jurisdictions. Federal funds are intended to cover up to 90 percent of local program costs (net of user payments), with the remainder provided locally in cash or in kind. Exceptions to this are programs for migrant workers and Indian families, where 100 percent federal financing is authorized. Up to 15 percent of federal funds may be used for grants or loans for construction of new facilities. The required fee schedule provides that children from two child families of income under $4320 receive services free of charge, that fees equal to 10 percent to 15 percent of income over $4320 are charged for children of families with income between $4320 and $7000 (the Bureau of Labor Statistics lower living standard budget), and that a sliding scale is to be set by HEW for children of families with incomes above the BLS standard. These payments, in conjunction with the federal grant money from the prime sponsor and the project's nonfederal matching share, are to be used to pay total project costs.

At the federal level, a Special Committee on Federal Standards for Child Development and Family Services is to be established to promulgate a new set of standards consistent with the Federal Interagency Day Care Requirements. Again, the membership must consist at least half of parents of children participating in the day care programs supported by the act. The standards which this committee establishes must be approved by the Secretary of HEW and apply to all programs providing child development and family services under the act.

Another special committee is to be established at the federal level for the purpose of developing a uniform minimum code for physical (building) facilities; the code is to be used in local licensing of child care facilities receiving funds under the act. The committee is to be made up of parents of participating children, officials of state and local licensing agencies, experts on public health, fire, construction, etc., and representatives of agencies administering various child care programs. Parents of children in programs under this act, the Economic Opportunity Act, and the Social Security Act are to make up at least half of the committee. States and localities would be urged to adopt these standards.

Further, the act requires the Secretary of HEW to establish an Office of Child Development, one purpose of which is to coordinate all child development and family service programs within HEW. Also, a Child Development Research Council is to be established to coordinate child development and family service-related activities under different federal agencies. The council is to include representatives of the Office of Child Development, the offices administering the Social Security Act and the Elementary and Secondary Education Act, the National Institute of Child Health and Human Development, the Office of Economic Opportunity, the Department of Labor, and other appropriate agencies.

The act outlines an organizational framework that would appear to accommodate our analysis of earlier chapters. Our notion of a community planning body, responsible for local planning and co-ordination of day care, seems consistent with the type of agency (local government department or nonprofit corporation) that would be designated by a prime sponsor to administer the provisions of the act. The principles of parent and citizen overview and participation are accommodated by the Child and Family Service Councils and project policy committees stipulated by the act. The provisions for income-related subsidies and voluntary use of day care conform to the rationale which we feel is justified for public support of day care. While sympathetic with the broad sweep of this proposed legislation, and many of its details, we would like in the remainder of this chapter to discuss what we feel are of some important problems of omission and commission.

The Quantity/Quality Trade-off

We are concerned that the Child Development Act does not really come to grips with the quantity/quality trade-off problem in subsidized day care. As suggested earlier there are strong pressures under a day care policy developed in the welfare context to deny resources to children in day care. But under the child development legislation there is an opposite tendency toward high expenditures per subsidized child, a policy that leads, in the context of limited federal appropriations, to separation of the potential users of day care (even within income categories) into two groups—those that receive resource intensive day care subsidized by the federal government, and those that receive much less resource intensive care with no federal subsidy or who can find no satisfactory extra-family arrangements.

The quantity/quality trade-off must be faced squarely, but at the present time it seems to be virtually ignored.

The basic question is this: Should federal subsidy involve large expenditure per child, in which case it is highly unlikely that the subsidy will be able to cover all children? Or should federal subsidy per child be smaller, but coverage greater? We have argued a case for a "moderate" subsidy per child, and wide coverage. It needs to be stressed, of course, that since federal subsidy will induce some mothers to work who otherwise would not, there is a governmental responsibility to provide reasonable assurance that subsidized day care is not generally inferior to the care the children would have gotten at home. But beyond such a basic level of care, the quantity/quality trade-off remains as an essential policy issue.

As it stands, the act creates pressure for high-quality, high-cost day care services, at the expense of wider coverage, in several different ways. First, the act contains explicit language on the subject. In particular, the act provides that "In no event shall any prime sponsor or program or project . . . reduce the quality of services . . . below the standards . . . in order to reduce expenditures per child or to extend services to large numbers of children." Second, the act delegates substantial authority to councils of parents and citizens at the project, local prime sponsor, state, and federal levels. The majorities on these councils—parents of participating children plus citizens with child care expertise—have interests in raising the standards and expenditure levels per child for *ongoing* day care programs supported by the act. On the other hand, the parents of children *not served* by the act are not directly represented. The constituency for quality, therefore, is stronger than the constituency for availability. Third, the language of the act suggests that public and private *nonprofit* agencies are to be given preference for project funding. While this general approach seems healthy, a heavy handed administration of such policy, featuring across-the-board rejection of private profitmaking supply, could exacerbate the bias toward high-cost programs and aggravate problems of supply adjustment.

Certainly fuller discussions of the issues involved here are needed. Because of the sharp split in philosophy between those who have argued for day care in the context of the Family Assistance Program and those who have argued for it in the context of the Child Development Act, concern about keeping day care costs within reason has tended to be labeled as "anti-child" by those who see day care as a service for children. This issue, as we see it, is that unless day care costs are restrained, only a limited number of children will be able to benefit from federal day care policy. Words like "custodial" and "developmental" day care have been thrown around rather loosely. The key question is, for what cost can adequate day care, care that makes children better (or at least no worse) off, be provided? In Chapter 4 we noted the limited evidence that such quality care will still be expensive, hopefully under $2000. Until subsidized care is widely available, expenditures must be kept to such levels, and not be allowed to inflate to the levels 50 percent and 100 percent higher, sometimes touted for fancier care. In addition, voluntary resources and user fees must be utilized effectively to keep actual governmental outlays per child within bounds. Otherwise the cost of providing very expensive day care will be borne largely by the children who will not find subsidized day care places. This question of the quantity/quality trade-off ought to be central in the continuing deliberation of the policymakers and parent-citizen councils of the prime sponsors, and of the individual day care projects themselves.

The act is farsighted in providing for regular surveys and analyses of needs for child development and family services by prime sponsors. Such efforts should be designed to make the quantity/quality issue explicit. The kind of opinion-polling methodology, discussed in Chapter 5, which probed the community's current usage and requirements for day care, what parents felt was important about day care, and what they would be willing to pay would seem to us an important planning and policy tool. Certainly, indications of present quality and usage patterns compared to the size and location of target groups for day care will give policymakers an appreciation of where the community stands on the quantity/quality trade-off issue. Furthermore, information on parent preferences and willingness to pay can serve as a guide in determining where the community *should* stand on this matter, insofar as parental judgments, as well as "expert opinion," are considered in establishing quality choices.

In addition, the willingness to pay information is quite useful in another way. For having families pay certain fractions of day care costs can be exploited as a force in restraining the growth of these costs. For this reason, we think it important that the councils contain parents who pay a significant fraction of day care costs as well as those that do not.

Because special facilities need not be provided or constructed, and transportation requirements to these more localized facilities may be smaller, one might expect that day care in family day care homes would be less costly than day care in specially provided day care centers. Evidence from the Mt. Pleasant interview study suggests both that many parents would be happy with day care provided in a home setting and that many parents might be willing to participate in the provision of family home day care. Although limited evidence from the Abt study indicates that cost savings that "good quality" homes would achieve over "good quality" centers may not be very substantial,[3] an evolving day care system might rest considerable weight on family day care homes, and we see no reason why federal subsidy should not go to such facilities. But while the language of the act is sufficiently broad to allow subsidy of day care homes, some of the act's provisions—such as the rigid fee schedules and the required structure of project policy committees—are more appropriate for centers than homes. Greater flexibility on this account seems desirable, both in the language of the act and in its ultimate administration.

The position of the act relative to proprietary day care is fairly benign. The act would leave this segment of the industry untouched except for patronage lost to newly subsidized nonprofit centers. In some cases, private profitmaking firms which agree to conform to the requirements of the act may actually be subsidized, although this will depend largely on the attitudes of the prime sponsor and its Child and Family Service Council. However, some child development advocates take a more extreme position, favoring forceful elimination of proprietary day care through stringent regulations. We think this would be a mistake. While we have serious misgivings about traditional private enterprise as the mode for organizing day care, in the absence of low-priced day care slots for all children who need it, one should be leary about stamping out one source of supply. While regulatory problems may be severe, in addition to expanding the supply of day care, the proprietary centers conceivably could serve a useful role in providing some alternative cost figures and bench marks.

The Coordination of Day Care Programs

Our second major concern with the act is its failure to address the problems of coordinating public sector programs and functions. It is utopian to expect passage of "a single umbrella" day care act in the near future. The many different lobby groups for day care virtually guarantee that there will be a variety of different pieces of legislation, sources of funds, and programs. However, we do think that attempts should be made to rectify this situation as much as possible.

The Child Development Act essentially grafts a new program onto the existing array of federal child care-related programs. Other than calling for establishment of a Child Development Research Council with members representing the different federal agencies administering child care programs, and requiring local sponsors to submit plans for coordinating their efforts with other agencies, the act does little to promote consolidation of the federal effort. For example, the act totally ignores 4-C as a possible source of help in this effort. And while the act takes an essential step towards facilitating the coordination, by designating the local prime sponsors as focal points for project applications, it fails to *direct other* grants programs under the Social Security Act, legislation administered by the Department of Labor, Model Cities, and other sources (potentially including the Family Assistance Plan) through this channel. In essence, these other programs would operate independently of the prime sponsor system, purchasing and providing day care services of their own, continuing to segregate children of parents on welfare or work training in centers providing separately from the act, and continuing the proliferation of different matching and eligibility requirements that discourage potential suppliers, reduce the effectiveness of overall federal funding, and dampen the vitality of the day care sector.

Given the political realities it is naive to assume that other child care programs can immediately be subsumed by the new act. However, some greater efforts toward coordination and consolidation seem warranted to improve administrative efficiency and provide for continuity of care when the training, employment, and income status of the parents change. A first major step would be to amend the other legislation applying to day care so that all programs work through the same prime sponsor system. (Alternatively, a wider perspective could be taken to coordinate day care programs with other child-related programs and with the still wider array of federal human service programs. This is, in fact, the objective of the Allied Service Act proposed by the administration in 1972.) Expenditures for child care and child placement actions, under the Social Security Act and other programs, could be channeled through the prime sponsor agency. In essence this would reduce the roles of other public agencies administering child care programs to purchasers of services for their clients. Other functions, such as grants for capital construction or standards enforcement, could be transferred to the prime sponsor agency also. This would mitigate many of the information and financing problems of both suppliers and parents by providing a common intermediary for transactions.

The other major problem of coordination comes at the local level where day care projects must comply with local licensing requirements as well as various federal program standards and qualifications. We saw in Chapter 3 how such a system may be ineffective for quality control purposes while it drains the vigor of local day care supply.

The act provides for the development of a set of uniform federal facility standards which states and localities are urged to adopt. However, it seems naive if not inappropriate and unnecessary to require state and local governments to change their health and safety codes to conform with federal regulations. What is required is prime sponsor agency responsibility for helping project applicants carry through local facility licensing procedures, and reducing the number of different governmental "windows" a project applicant must visit in order to complete the necessary prerequisites for operation. Several alternatives are possible. For example, the prime sponsor agency charged with administering the provisions of the act (our community planning body) could simply provide technical assistance in the form of information and advice to project applicants; a more forceful approach would be for that agency to serve as intermediary in performing, or arranging to have carried out, the licensing and inspection functions of building, fire, and health departments for day care facilities. Such coordinating procedures could be required for inclusion in prime sponsor program statements submitted to HEW.

Planning and Choice

Integration and coordination of federally supported day care programs clearly is essential if we are to develop machinery for rational allocation of day care resources. In the absence of such coordination it is difficult to see how resources are to flow to where the needs are greatest. Even with such coordination it is important not to underestimate the difficulty of the planning function. The data requirements for guiding allocation are not inconsiderable. In Chapter 5 we discussed the nature of those requirements and a possible mechanism for obtaining data. In Chapter 4 we suggested that a community planning body, e.g., the local government prime sponsor agency, take charge of the planning and coordinating functions.

Even with a coordinated set of programs and well-working planning machinery, however, we think it would be a mistake to run a system of publicly supported day care facilities in such a way as to give parents no choice among alternative day care facilities. We think it a bad idea to assign children to particular centers. Indeed our proposals for organization put substantial emphasis on consumer choice as a mechanism for evaluating day care operations. Our concern here goes beyond that expressed above regarding ascription of children to particular centers according to the particular federal program applicable to their circumstances. Here we are talking about the more straightforward kind of ascription by residential location that has marked the public school system. We see no convincing reason why such a policy should be adopted in day care. It seems incongruous that at a time when school systems are moving to extend the range of choice for children and parents at the elementary school level we develop a system of national day care where such freedom of choice is excluded. The reasons for freedom of choice and some mechanisms to make it effective, were discussed at length earlier. Freedom of choice cannot substitute for a planning and regulatory structure but it can be an extremely important complement to such a structure in keeping the day care program on its toes and keeping parents and children content.

Conclusion

Despite our criticisms and suggestions, the child development legislation would be an important and positive beginning in the construction of a smoothly functioning universal day care delivery system. Our comments are offered basically in terms of urging constructive modifications rather than in suggesting major changes in the concept. To the contrary, over the longrun we would urge a consolidation of the various child care programs under the framework of such an act.

One of our main concerns is with the ability of the day care sector to allocate resources effectively. This requires an awareness on the part of local citizens and federal officials of communities' outstanding needs for day care, as well as the quality of ongoing programs. Effective data gathering, planning, and evaluation by prime sponsor agencies, complemented by the machinery of consumer choice and citizen overview and participation, is required.

The need for evaluation and assessment is not confined to the question of allocation, narrowly conceived in terms of standards and availability of care. One is also interested in what kinds of day care arrangements prove to be generally more satisfactory and reliable in providing care of an economic but healthful and developmental nature. Such information will be invaluable for project selection by local agencies and individual parents, over the longrun. The Child Development Act would provide research and development funds for HEW to use for experimenting with and evaluating new program approaches and disseminating this information. We would urge that research not be confined to assessment of techniques in child care and teaching preschoolers, but also to evaluating the kinds of agencies—profitmaking, voluntary, and the like—which most consistently provide effective care. For while we have stated our understanding of this question within the bounds of existing knowledge and theory, we by no means close the book on further inquiry. Finding new and better forms of service organization will be essential to stimulating and preserving the vitality of day care over the long run.

Notes

Chapter 1
Introduction

1. Gwen Morgan, private communication.
2. Representative Shirley Chisolm, Hearings of the Select Sub-committee on Education and Labor, U.S. House of Representatives, 1969.
3. See Greta G. Fein and Linda K. Moore, *Day Care in Context* unpublished manuscript, Yale University, 1971, Chapter I, "Day Care in Context Past and Present."
4. See Stevanne Auerbach, "History of Day Care Services," Hearings on *Comprehensive Preschool Education and Child Day Care Act of 1969*, U.S. House of Representatives, 1969.

Chapter 2
The Demand and Supply of Extra-Family Day Care

1. President Richard M. Nixon, Economic Opportunity Amendments of 1971–Veto Message (H. Doc. No. 92-48), December 8, 1971.
2. This at $650 per child. The basic data are from *Day Care Survey of 1970* (Westinghouse Learning Corporation for the Office of Economic Opportunity). Henceforth this study will be referred to as the Westinghouse study. The Office of Child Development recommends a day care program that cost roughly three times this figure.
3. T.P. Schultz, "An Economic Model of Family Planning and Fertility," *Journal of Political Economy* (1969).
4. The mortality figures and the data on children per woman are taken from *Historical Statistics of the United States* and the *Statistical Abstracts of the United States.* These are our basic demographic references.
5. For a discussion see R. Wells, "Demographic Change in the Life Cycle for American Families from the 18th to the 20th Centuries," paper presented at the Population Association of America, April 23, 1971, Washington, D.C.

6. Westinghouse Study, op. cit.

7. This analysis is implicit in G. Steiner, *The State of Welfare* (The Brookings Institution, 1971). It is virtually certain that a national program of subsidized day care would involve costs of well over $1000 per child, far above the $650 average reported in Westinghouse.

8. *Historical Statistics of the United States* and *Statistical Abstracts of the United States.*

9. J. Mincer, "Labor Force Participation of Married Women: A Study of Labor Supply," *Aspects of Labor Economics* (National Bureau of Economic Research, Princeton University Press, 1967).

10. For an excellent discussion of the history of day care see G. Fein and A. Clarke-Stewart, *Day Care in Context* (forthcoming), as well as Chapter 1 of this volume.

11. For a more detailed account see Steiner, op. cit., and Chapter 3 of this volume.

12. F. Low and T. Spindler, *Child Care Arrangements of Working Mothers in the United States* (U.S. Department of Health, Education and Welfare, Children's Bureau Publication No. 461, 1968).

13. R. Zamoff and L. Vogt, *Assessment of Day Care Services and Needs at the Community Level* (Urban Institute, 1971).

14. R. Zamoff and J. Lyle, "Assessment of Day Care Services and Needs at the Community Level: Mt. Pleasant," Urban Institute Paper 714-1-1, November 1971.

15. Gwen Morgan, private communication.

16. A study of day care costs which attempted to take these factors into account was made by Abt Associates for the Office of Economic Opportunity; see Abt Associates, Inc., *A Study in Child Care 1970-1971* (4 vols.) (Cambridge, Mass.: 1971).

Chapter 3
**The Present System of Publicly Supported
Day Care**

1. See *Special Analysis of the United States Government*, Fiscal Year 1973, p. 144. These figures are for full-day care and do not include part-day Headstart and other preschool education programs.

2. This section benefits heavily from information documented in

Patricia G. Bourne et al., "Day Care Nightmare," Working Paper No. 145, Institute of Urban and Regional Development, University of California at Berkeley, February 1971.

3. Community Nutrition Institute, *CNI Weekly Report* 2, 27 (October 5, 1972), Washington, D.C.

4. Estimates of the D.C. Department of Human Resources.

5. Kirschner Associates, Inc., "A Preliminary Survey of the Quality of Day Care in the District of Columbia," January 1971.

6. Private communication.

7. Ibid.

8. Quoted from Abt Associates report, op. cit.

9. Quoted from Patricia G. Bourne, op. cit.

10. For a recent evaluation of the 4-C program see "Report of the Panel on the Assessment of the Community Coordinated Child Care Program," Division of Behavioral Sciences, National Research Council, National Academy of Sciences, 1972.

11. Quoted from Patricia G. Bourne, op. cit.

12. See Mary Dublin Keyserling, *Windows on Day Care, A Report on the Findings of Members of the National Committee of Jewish Women on Day Care Needs and Services in their Communities*, New York, 1972.

Chapter 4
Two Major Issues of Public Policy: Public Subsidy and Organization of Supply

1. There seems no point in working out the details of a cost/benefit analysis here. For various calculations see Steiner, op. cit.

2. See Charles L. Schultze, Edward R. Fried, Alice M. Rivlin, Nancy H. Teeters, *Setting National Priorities: The 1973 Budget*, "Child Care," Chapter 8 (The Brookings Institution, 1972), pp. 252-90.

3. Christopher Jencks et al., *Inequality: A Reassessment of the Effect of Family and Schooling in America* (New York: Basic Books, 1972).

In a private communication Dr. Julius B. Richmond has noted that more recent studies are indicating some long-term gains associated with Headstart, particularly in cases where parent involvement seems to be effective.

4. A precise discussion of expenditure level would have to account for the value of unpaid resources used in day care. Pricing of nonmonetized resources such as volunteer labor or rent-free space provided by a charitable institution is a tricky economic question. On the one hand, the costs of using such resources are not zero—there are usually alternative uses to which these resources may be put. On the other hand, it would be an overestimation to value such resources at the rate at which analogous resources sell in the marketplace. The appropriate questions to ask are: What would a volunteer citizen do if he or she were not volunteering in a day care center? How would a church use its space during the work day, if not for day care?

There is the further consideration that if day care services grow rapidly, then the supply of volunteer labor and facilities may become exhausted and resources will then have to be purchased. Thus expenditure figures estimated in the context of present (volunteer) conditions would underestimate future requirements, unless new sources of volunteer resources could be tapped. In summary, therefore, it seems sensible to price unpaid resources substantially below market prices, until supply limits are approached.

5. Abt Associates, op. cit.

6. See F. Ruderman, "Child Care and Working Mothers" (Child Welfare League of America, 1958). In particular, see Table 12, p. 78.

7. The flavor comes through strongly in Ruderman.

8. For a discussion of this point of view see Fein and Clarke-Stewart, op. cit.

9. See Ruderman, op. cit.

10. A. Hirschman, *Exit, Voice and Loyalty* (Cambridge: Harvard University Press, 1970).

11. A. Downs, "Competition and Community Schools," in *Urban Problems and Prospects* (Markham Press, 1970).

12. See Gayle Tunnell, "Day Care Technology: Growing Field," *Washington Post*, March 2, 1971.

13. See Chapter 5 and Zamoff and Vogt, op. cit.

14. Gwen Morgan, private communication.

15. The interviews were conducted by Emma Jackson. See Chapter 3.

Chapter 5
Planning and Evaluation of Day Care at
the Community Level

1. See R. Zamoff and J. Lyle, "Who Needs What Kind of Day Care Center," *Child Welfare* (New York: Child Welfare League of America. June 1973).

2. Of course, census data will not provide clues as to resident priorities for various types of day care arrangements. Since census data are made available on a tract, enumeration district, or block basis, it is impossible to perform statistical analyses that depend upon individual data. And since census data are collected only once every ten years, they could become out of date relatively rapidly.

3. Some of this information is available for the total population while other information is based on a 5, 20 or 25 percent sample from which valid generalizations can be drawn.

4. For examples of such interviews see Richard B. Zamoff, "Guide to the Assessment of Day Care Services and Needs at the Community Level," Urban Institute Paper, 1205-5, July 1971.

5. According to C&P Telephone Company information, the proportion of households in the Model Neighborhood and in Mt. Pleasant without telephones is about the same as the rest of the District of Columbia—about 15 percent. However, there are other neighborhoods in Washington, D.C., in which as many as 25 percent of the households are without phones.

6. The neighborhood resident telephone interview form and supplementary material used in the Urban Institute's day care studies have been translated into Spanish.

7. For a copy of the interview form, see Zamoff, op. cit.

8. This discussion is based on the experience gained in the Urban Institute day care studies, and on Carol Weiss and Harry P. Hatry, *An Introduction to Sample Surveys for Government Managers* (Urban Institute, March 1971), pp. 23-24.

9. While this appears to suggest that the (screened) sample was not large enough, a greatly enlarged sample might still have neglected to pick up many day care center users. Only 5 percent of all children under age six currently could be accommodated by available day care center slots in Mt. Pleasant.

10. For such interviews see Zamoff, op. cit.

Chapter 6
National Day Care Policy

1. U.S. Senate version, Comprehensive Headstart, Child Development and Family Services Act, May 1972.
2. See Steiner, op. cit.
3. Abt Associates, op. cit.

Index

Index

ABT study, 41
AFDC, 24, 27-30, 32, 33, 35, 43, 44
Abt Associates, 53
Agnes Meyer Foundation, 34
Aide to Families With Dependent
  Children, *see* AFDC
Allied Service Act, 101
Assessment method, 76-90

BHZ, 38, 39
Babysitting, 16-17
Bethany Day Nursery, 1
Birth rates, 11-12
Bureau of Building Housing and
  Zoning, *see* BHZ
Bureau of Community and Institution-
  al Hygiene, 38, 39
Bureau of Labor Statistics, 95

CEP, 43
CHSA, 35, 36
California, 29
Catholic Charities, 41
Child development *passim; and see*
  Child Development Act; Child Devel-
  opment Research Council; Child
  Welfare Services; Comprehensive
  Child Development Act; Office of
  Child Development
Child Development Act, 91-92, 93-96,
  96-97, 100
Child Development Research Council,
  96, 100
Child and Family Service Councils, 68,
  93-94, 96, 99
Child Welfare Services, 24-25, 34
Childbearing, age of mothers at, 11-12
Civil War, 2
Community Action Agency Program,
  26
Community Coordinated Child Care
  (4-C) Program, *see* 4-C
Community Health Centers, 26
Community Health Services Adminis-
  tration, *see* CHSA
Comprehensive Child Development
  Act, xiv, 4
Comprehensive Headstart, Child Devel-
  opment, and Family Services Act,
  see Child Development Act

Concentrated Employment Program,
  25, 35
Cooperatives, 60-62
Coordination, 36-40, 66-67, 100-101
Cubans, 26

DCD, 38, 39, 43
D.C. City Council, 38
D.C. Community Health Services
  Administration, 32
D.C. Department of Human Resources, 32, 38, 68
DLS, 38, 39
Day care: delivery system for, xiv, 7;
  demand for, 10-16, 76-81; eligibility
  policies for, 6, 7, 27-28; federal
  support for, 2-3, 12, 16, 20, 21-46;
  fee schedules for, 6, 17, 18-19; his-
  tory of in U.S., 1-2; organization of,
  xiv, 62-67; planning and evaluation
  at community level, 71-90; present
  system of, 21-46, 40-45; public
  support for, xiii-xiv, 2-3, 8, 19, 20;
  quality standards for, 6-7, 20, 45;
  subsidy schedules, 6-7, 48-55; supply
  of, 16-20, 66-67, 81-84
Delivery system for day care, xiv, 7
Demand for day care, 10-16, 76-81
Dental care, 54
Department of Agriculture, 30
Department of Commerce, 30
Department of Defense, 30
Department of Housing and Urban
  Development, 30, 34
Department of the Interior, 26, 30
Department of Labor, 30, 35, 96, 100
Department of Licensing and Inspec-
  tion, 35-36
Depression, 2
District of Columbia, *see* Washington,
  D.C.
Division of Child Development, *see*
  DCD
Division of Licensing and Standards,
  see DLS

Economic Opportunity Act, 25, 26,
  95
Education Impact Aid, 26
Education, preschool, 2, 3

113

Quality Standards for day care centers, 6-7, 20, 45
Quantity-quality trade-off, 96-99

Regional Committee, 26, 34

Schultz, T.P., 11
Settlement House, 15
Single parents, *see* One-parent households
SRS, 28, 30
SSA, 33, 34, 35
Social and Rehabilitation Service, *see* SRS
Social Rehabilitation Administration, 39
Social Security Act, 24-25, 95, 96, 100, 101
Social Services Administration, *see* SSA
Special Committee on Federal Standards for Child Development and Family Services, 95
Steiner, G., 17
Subsidy schedules for day care centers, 6-7, 48-55
Suppliers, 44-45
Supply of day care centers, 16-20, 66-67, 81-84; organization of, 55-62

Title IA, *see* Headstart
Title IB, *see* Concentrated Employment Program

Title IVA, *see* AFDC
Title IVB, *see* Child Welfare Services
Title IVC, *see* WIN

United Fund, 29
United Givers Fund, 33, 41
United Planning Organization, 34
Urban Institute, 71
Urban Renewal, 26

Virginia Nursery, 1

WIN, 4, 24, 33, 35, 43
WPA, 2, 3
War production, 3
Washington, D.C.: day care in, 31-40, 71; Health and Welfare Council, 34, 35; Model Neighborhood, 16; *and see* Mt. Pleasant neighborhood
Welfare, xiii, xiv, 3, 4, 5, 28, 92
Welfare Department, 28, 29
Westinghouse survey, 12, 17, 18, 19, 51, 52, 59
Willingness to pay and community resources, 84-88
Women's liberation, xiii, 3, 4
Work Incentive Program, *see* WIN
Working mothers, 3, 4, 12, 14-15, 16, 32, 78, 79, 92, 94
World War I, 2
World War II, 2, 3

Zamoff and Vogt study, 16

About the Authors

Dennis Young is currently a member of the faculty of the Program for Urban and Policy Sciences at the State University of New York at Stony Brook and a consultant to the Urban Public Finance Group of the Urban Institute. Formerly he was a member of the senior research staff of the Urban Institute where he developed and directed a project on the economic organization of public services. His principal research interest is in this area, including work in the areas of urban sanitation, day care, criminal justice, and education. Dr. Young received the B.A. and M.A. degrees in electrical engineering from the City College of New York and Stanford University, respectively, and the Ph.D. in the Engineering-Economic Systems Department at Stanford University.

Richard R. Nelson is professor of Economics at Yale University. He received the B.A. from Oberlin College and the Ph.D. from Yale University. He has served on the staffs of The Rand Corporation and the Council of Economic Advisors.